The Portland Police

SUNSHINE DIVISION

An Early History

Lori Shea Kuechler

SUNSHINE DIVISION, INC.

Historical photographs are courtesy of the agencies and individuals credited.

International Standard Book Number 0-99742364-0-3

Library of Congress Control Number 2003094921

Editorial and production assistance:

Graphic Arts Center Publishing Company, Portland, Oregon

Cover design: Vicki Knapton

Interior book design and editing: Jean Andrews

Production: Dick Owsiany, Vicki Knapton

Printing: Haagen Printing

Book binding: Lincoln & Allen Co.

Printed and bound in the United States of America

Published by Sunshine Division, Inc.

687 North Thompson Street

Portland, Oregon 97227-1820

(503) 823-2119

www.sunshinedivision.org

The book is dedicated

to the extraordinary citizenry

of Portland, Oregon, who have allowed

the Police Bureau to be far more important

to the basic welfare of its people

than any city has ever dared.

THIS PUBLICATION MADE
POSSIBLE THANKS TO THE
GENEROUS SUPPORT OF:

WEST COAST BANK

Service is our Signature.

CONTENTS

ACKNOWLEDGMENTS

I would like to acknowledge the support and love of my best friend and husband, Sunshine Division Commander Sergeant Wayne Kuechler, who stops the car for every half-buried historical marker between here and wherever we go. I am happy to admit that his passion for local history has become my own.

Without the cooperation, enthusiasm, and expertise of the staff of the Stanley Parr Archive and Record Center of the City of Portland, there would be little primary documentation for this manuscript. Brian "Splendid" Johnson and Diana Banning hold and protect the records—and therefore the history of the city of Portland with skill and insight. I am pleased that the Sunshine Division Collection is now safe in their hands, and I encourage city of Portland bureaus to entrust their historical documents to SPARC for long-term safekeeping and accessibility.

I am so thankful for the willingness of Jean Andrews, Vicki Knapton, and Dick Owsiany of Graphic Arts Center Publishing Company to work with a wet-nose like me. I felt like a topnotch author during the entire experience.

In High and Far-Off times, my father, James Robert Shea, satisfied my insatiable curiosity with tales of the great grey-green, greasy Limpopo River, all set about with fever-trees. For that, I am most politely and forever his.

And finally, I am deeply indebted to the community of Warner Pacific College, particularly Dr. Cole Dawson without whom I would never have dared to write a book. Cole, I am beginning to understand that faith and scholarship do indeed lead to service.

FROM THE AUTHOR

In 1927, the hands of Mrs. C. H. Tichenor, wife of the first official commander of the Sunshine Division, moved quickly over layered padding and donated fabrics. Her passion for the needs of the poor combined with her skill as a quilter created fine bed-coverings for those who could not afford to heat their homes. I cannot quilt, so I will write.

As the wife of the current commander, I hope I have brought forth something that will do justice to the early history of the Portland Police Sunshine Division. Much like a quilter, but far less skilled in my craft than Mrs. Tichenor in hers, mine is an attempt to gather thousands of tiny, worn-out pieces carefully saved for practical use. I hope that I have stitched together a cohesive covering, and that my sentimentality does not render the writing unscholarly, nor my objectivity render it without soul. I suppose in my case, since I am both personally and historically involved, I should expect that both might occur from time to time.

In spite of my level of skill or sentimentality, I hope it will be understood that the Portland Police Sunshine Division has quietly and respectfully fed, clothed, and warmed hundreds of thousands of people for the last eighty years. Of that fact, the data renders no dispute. From any perspective, it is captivating to realize that if you live in Portland, Oregon, and you find yourself suddenly unable to feed your family—call the police.

—Lori Shea Kuechler

1

THE POOR MAN BESIDE ME

I ought not to allow any man, because he has broad lands,
to feel that he is rich in my presence.
I ought to make him feel that I can do without his riches,
that I cannot be bought—neither by comfort neither by pride,
and though I be utterly penniless, and receiving bread from him,
that he is the poor man beside me.
—*Man the Reformer,* Ralph Waldo Emerson[1]

When Harry A. Circle left the grocery business and joined the Portland Police Bureau on May 8, 1903, there were fifty-five members on the city's force. In his time, the officers were clothed in long, brass-buttoned coats and derbylike helmets. They walked late-night beats or rode horseback, sometimes for twelve hours a day, seven days a week.[2] By his retirement in June 1952, the seventy-eight-year-old Captain Circle had served the city as an interurban operator, a record clerk, the head clerk, a bailiff, a patrolman, a precinct captain, a captain of the Auxiliary, a captain of detectives, and as a somewhat unorthodox St. Nicholas.

Beginning in the winter of 1917, a small wooden box on Captain Circle's desk housed a thin layer of pocket change. The money was used to feed the poor. His men always carried change. If the captain did not procure the change, the officer might spend it on lunch, but not usually, as restaurants generally refused payment in hopes that the officer might return as a "built-in" security measure.

Quite often, the policeman on the street gave his change to whoever needed it—as deemed by the officer. At times it went to someone who should "move along," or someone who needed a meal, or both. Captain Circle preferred that the change might find its way into the box on his desk.

Capt. H. A. Circle (SPARC, A2002-009)

Not wanting to discourage their generosity, Captain Circle brought the donation box to their attention. He believed that the men on the street carried a unique and private insight into the needs of the community, but they were not compensated enough to support every concern without the cooperation of like-minded peers. And perhaps he felt that the act of giving gave the officers a chance to see themselves more fully as public servants.

As the layer of coins thickened, the proceeds were selectively used for the purchase of groceries, provisions, and clothing for families that had been identified as being in need. In addition, hungry families received basket deliveries at Christmastime. By 1920 and 1921, Captain Circle's officers established a routine in which those in need were casually discovered, discussed, and assisted during the daily rounds of the policemen of the downtown headquarters.

Therefore, in reality and in spirit, the first Portland Police person of authority to organize officers in the collection and distribution of food for the poor was Captain Circle. The charitable work of Captain Circle and his benevolent following received its first smattering of publicity in December 1921, fatefully due to the very social Mrs. Circle and her fund-raising card party.

Behind Every Good Man . . .

Mrs. Circle discovered two small children in tattered overalls, with no coats or flannels, running and jumping about the playground of Woodlawn School.[3] Their father had passed away only two months earlier, leaving their mother alone to care for the family. What bothered Mrs. Circle the most—they were wearing no shoes.

She made inquiries regarding where they lived and, of course, sent her charitable husband to the children's house that evening. He discovered a young widow of poor health with six children aged five months to nine years who were very much in need. The next day, Captain Circle mentioned the family to his officers, subsequently sending his men "penniless" onto the streets after roll call.

According to Captain Circle, his officers were told, "It takes a lot to feed six youngsters all trying to grow up at the same time. And this mother is trying to do it on the small earnings she makes taking in washing."[4] The collection was unusually generous, but by that time, Mrs. Circle had already placed an announcement in the newspaper for a charitable card party to be held at the Woodman Hall on Seventh and Alder the following Tuesday.

Captain Circle contacted a few grocers and local businessmen asking for contributions to the family. "And say," quoted Captain Circle in his conclusion to the *Oregon Journal* reporter inspired by Mrs. Circle, "If you know anybody who has extra blankets, that family could use them mighty well. Nights are getting cold now." The family was clothed and fed that very cold winter of 1921, leaving extra for other families in need.

The year previous, although it had not been publicized, there is indication that officers made basket deliveries of Christmas dinners to a few impoverished families during the holiday season of 1920.[5] They handled their contributions and made the deliveries on their own time as well as during working hours. Chief Leon Jenkins did not appear to object to the deliveries on city time. Apparently, he harbored a hope that the effort of the officers might have an impact upon the perception of the police as well as lessen crimes committed due to Christmastime desperation.

The whole process was quite informal and spontaneous after the newspaper story of Captain and Mrs. Circle in 1921. Immediately following, Chief Jenkins observed the positive public response and instructed his officers to ". . . investigate conditions of poverty in their districts and to list those families deserving of aid,"[6] in hopes the officers might develop the community support they needed to extend their efforts. His assumptions were correct. The Portland Police Bureau rank and file, as well as local merchants, acknowledged, accepted, and supported the charitable effort of the policemen as an effective, preventive form of law enforcement.

It could be speculated that what is now considered Community Policing in Portland found its original expression in the winter of 1921. In a more practical sense—the sense that Captain Circle would probably prefer—these spontaneous acts of charity simply met the immediate needs of the people for whom the officers had concern. To the intrigued public, the generous nature of the officers gave insight to the struggle of compassionate policemen at a loss to interrupt the relationship between crime and poverty. Unique to Portland was the public willingness to participate in that dynamic.

Sgt. L. V. Jenkins (SPARC, A2002-009)

In a tiny newspaper article on Christmas Eve 1921, Chief of Police Leon Jenkins congratulated Captain Harry Circle for the manner in which he conducted the "collection of supplies for the twenty-six needy families that received Christmas dinners from the police on Friday." [7] He requested that the captain extend his expression of appreciation to the members of the force who assisted in the work.

In 1922, the charitable dynamics within the police department and the local willingness to contribute to their cause continued to unfold. In addition, the public relations dynamic of policemen serving the poor did not evade the opportunistic eye of a man quite different from Captain Circle. After the first of three reelections, "Peoples Mayor" George L. Baker, a politician with a flare for the conspicuous, was looking for every opportunity to link the business community with city government. As a new member of the political establishment of Portland, Baker needed to continue to tie himself into the merchant community. [8] Captain Circle's band of holiday givers naturally drew attention to the officers as compassionate figures of public authority, working alongside the local merchants as generous philanthropists.

The following chapters represent the story of three streams of community activity that create and sustain the Portland Police Sunshine Division. The first is the seemingly inherent and long-term tendency of the Portland Police Bureau to find creative ways to assist the poor—and the willingness of the city of Portland to sustain the activity. The second stream is the philanthropic and community-oriented volunteer activities of local business owners willing to donate time and resources to emergency relief. Third is the willingness of local newspapers and radio stations to offer publicity.

Although the establishing element in the story of the Sunshine Division is the initial action of a police captain who gave to those in desperate need, it is not nor will it ever be a unique phenomenon. Police officers often give pocket money for a runaway's trip home, or buy a late-night dinner for a young person in transport to Juvenile Detention Hall, as well as for an occasional set of clothes for a young child rescued from squalor.

What is unique to this story is that the police, the city, and the community of Portland, Oregon, have managed to weave themselves into an eighty-year act of kindness, out of respect for the poignant opportunities that law enforcement provides.

PORTLAND
RESERVE
68
POLICE

2

THE PORTLAND POLICE VIGILANTES

From 1917 to 1933, Mayor George Baker was a man of extreme patriotism and enthusiasm when the people of Portland, Oregon, believed it impossible to be too much of either. With an open door policy[1] and a propensity to strategically join or detach himself from any and every fraternal organization his political ambitions would allow, the "rags to riches" theater owner was known by the business community as "Our George."[2] Portland historian Carl Abbott writes that Baker ". . . believed in the flag, free enterprise, Allied victory in the World War, and the growth of a prosperous Portland where 'smokestacks will be as numerous as the trees in the forest.'"[3] In a 1917 campaign letter to hundreds of men throughout the city, Baker promised to be a hands-on administrator.[4]

My Dear Mr. G.

I have been very much encouraged in my campaign and if my friends continue their active support on my behalf until my election is over, there will be no question about my success. . . .

I will appreciate all the assistance you can give me in my campaign and if elected, "Welcome" will always be written on the door mat.

Sincerely yours,
Geo. L. Baker[5]

In fact, it always was—to those who offered their active support. To those who did not, Mayor Baker's "open door policy" had hinges. After running for office on a fervently patriotic platform riveted against industrial labor strife, Baker orchestrated police raids, designed to save the city from anarchy. The raids targeted what he called "Huns" (Germans), "Reds" (Southeastern Europeans), and particularly "Wobblies" (International Workers of the World).[6]

Although it is tempting to vilify George Baker, it might be more accurate to place him in context as a person chosen by the people. The state and the city in which he lived were an exception in an exceptional time, offering a formula for extremes. Historian E. Kimbark MacColl writes:

> *To understand the intensity of Oregon's response to the war, one must examine the roots of its population. Approximately 85 percent of the state's residents in 1917 were native born. The largest number had emigrated from the Middle West, with the second largest contingent from the South. The early New England influence, more of quality than of quantity was beginning to wane but the "covered wagon" complex was still prevalent. The pioneers had brought true Americanism with them and their descendents fought to preserve this purity in the face of an influx of foreign immigrants from the Orient and Southeastern Europe. With one of the most homogenous populations in the country, Oregon was overwhelmingly white, Anglo-Saxon and Protestant. . . .*
>
> *Under the stimulus of a well-prepared program of war propaganda, it was not difficult to transfer vaguely defined fears into a real live enemy. . . .*
>
> *. . . it was not surprising that Portland's established families fell right into line. Although not a part of this group, George Luis Baker provided just the touch of drama and authority that Portlanders relished. He personified Portland's dedicated support of President Woodrow Wilson's "Crusade for Democracy."*[7]

Mayor George Luis Baker, 1917–1933

In addition, as a result of his capacity for micromanagement in his areas of greatest concern, the Portland Police Bureau was blessed—but more often afflicted—with Mayor Baker's detailed attention. A logistic indication of his commitment to involve himself in every detail of police business emerged as the *Portland Telegram* reported that the mayor would be chief of police for "a month or so" while City Commissioner C. A. Bigelow would assume the mayor's other duties.

Mayor Baker feels, he says, that policemen have been trying earnestly to stem the wave of crime which has swept the city for the last few months but he believes with his presence at headquarters they will be stirred to greater effort and results will be forthcoming.[8]

In addition to his month as chief, by the end of 1921, Baker had visited several major cities on the West Coast in an attempt to understand the complexities unique to fast-growing, western municipalities. Along with the crime statistics associated with the complications of Prohibition, extraordinary growth and a relatively new local government placed intense demands on the administration of services. With an impish, inquisitive demeanor and familiarizing charm, Baker developed rapport with similar city governments up and down the West Coast to gain insights on the patterns of newly settled urban-growth areas.

Upon taking office as mayor of Portland, Baker faced the challenge of administrating a city in the midst of overwhelming expansion with insufficient municipal planning. Baker was intuitively aware that the people of his beloved city were a people who tended to require identifiable foes for which they could be rallied against. Quite often, his trouble-shooting approach was to form committees in the spirit of the Western posse.

In the 1922 Mayor's Address encapsulating the year 1921, Baker offered the success of the Federal Rail Rate Decision to reduce shipping rates to Portland as an example of business-oriented citizens rallying for a cause with a winning result.[9]

"Portland has been reaping the harvest from community campaigning and community aggressiveness sown during the last two to three years. Portland went out for the things that belonged to Portland and success has been the result as long as the spirit lasts. The rail rate decision, which was gained only by fighting, has brought a harvest of business which belonged to Portland but which formerly went elsewhere while Portland suffered. . . . This trade has been a big factor in keeping our mills working and our people employed.[10]

Baker represented Portland, to the country and to itself, as a roll-up-your-sleeves-and-work-together-kind-a-town—rural in ethic while economically savvy in deed.

Not long after Baker's return from his handshaking, fact-finding visits to the cities of Seattle and San Francisco, he was energized to implement his new ideas. At his disposal was a patriotically flavored public awareness of the need for effective law enforcement amidst the complexities of Prohibition and the postwar displacement of veterans and shipyard workers. He harbored big plans for economic development and community cooperation with civil order maintained peacefully by municipal law-enforcement personnel.

In the midst of his enthusiasm for a well-staffed Police Bureau, Baker's plans were stopped cold when the State Tax Commission presented a dramatically reduced 1922 budget for the Portland Police Department.[11] Seeing themselves vigilant for the citizens of the state, and therefore called to protect the people from a heavy tax burden, the commission decreased the police budget by $78,000 necessitating the reduction of the Police Bureau by forty sworn officers.

The commission's rationale was based upon the highly publicized suggestion of then–Portland Police Chief Leon Jenkins that the bureau modernize from foot patrol to the more efficient car and motorcycle patrol. Chief Jenkins's desire to lean away from foot patrols and bring technological advances to the Police Department was transformed by the Tax Commission into a budget reduction, thereby injuring his reputation with the mayor and the city.

The commission's suggestion (and therefore economic mandate) was to put the city into action with a new law-enforcement methodology called the "12-Booth Theory." With this method, "two men could cover the same ground that eight or more men could cover on foot." One officer would be stationed at a communications booth and the other would patrol the district by car or motorcycle while checking in at the booth every fifteen minutes. The theory was largely untested but gaining functional popularity and refinement in law enforcement circles throughout the nation; it would eventually revolutionize law enforcement in densely populated areas.[12]

In a direct and terse response to the powerful State Tax Commission, Baker took his stand.

> *Although I can do nothing in the face of the action of the committee except to get along the best I can with what is left me, I still reserve the right to criticize and think that there never was a city confronted with a more absurd and farcical situation. . . . I am not going to*

establish and try out the new booth system unless ways and means are provided.[13]

"Ways and means" indirectly described the predicted need for additional cars and motorcycles—something the Tax Commission had overlooked. Baker rightfully feared the reduced police force would be spread throughout the city in twelve locations without sufficient transportation or backup. In addition, reduced numbers of law enforcement personnel could not as effectively isolate, surround, and put down a workers' riot—or any other kind of riot for that matter.

Adding fuel to the public support for Baker's outrage over the "12-Booth Theory," nearly all of the removed officers would be veterans of the war in Europe, hired by Baker as a token of gratitude for the service they had given to their country. Baker, as well as the Portland business community, viewed the layoff of exservicemen from paid duty as an atrocity and a betrayal of the worst kind.

Baker's response to the situation captured public sentiment as well as the first sworn members of the Portland Vigilance Police. Falling just short of accusing the Tax Commission of falling into the hands of Bootleggers, Wobblies, and Huns, he responded with a citizen call to arms.

. . . To do that now would cut forty more men from the force and would wipe out every exservice man we have with us—the newest and best blood on the force. I will not risk crippling the department to that extent to try out a new theory of policing. The special service on bootlegging and morals work cannot be reduced. The minute we reduce there and take men off, vice swarms out of its holes and pours in on us from other cities where policing is more rigid. We will if necessary, call upon the citizens to give subsidiary volunteer service through the winter months when the police problem is most severe. I propose to develop a vigilance committee consisting of one hundred private citizens to help handle the situation.[14]

Thus, in a dynamic response to budget reductions in police services, the idea for the Portland Police Vigilance Reserve was born. Baker's huge popularity, patriotism, and rapport with city business owners made his plea serious. By the end of the week, Mayor Baker announced the future appointment of a colorful and high-profile inspector (the contemporary equivalent to a detective) named C. H. Tichenor to head the vigilance committee.

Inspector C. H. Tichenor

Carroll Holt Tichenor received his appointment to the Portland Police Bureau in January 1902. First, he had charge of the old City Rock Pile (yes, it is acceptable to imagine men chained together in stripped suits smashing rocks with hammers under Tichenor's supervision). Next he drove the one and only patrol wagon, then he "walked a beat" in the north end of downtown when that district was "plenty tuff." Next he was a jailer, until he was assigned to the Mounted Division; as such, when President Teddy Roosevelt visited Portland, Tichenor was assigned as his personal bodyguard. Following his service as a mounted officer, he was promoted to the Detective Division, where he served fifteen years during which time he handled a number of important murder cases.[15]

Detective Sergeant C. H. Tichenor

Newspapers of the 1920s often made swashbuckling heroes out of local detectives and sheriffs. Inspector Tichenor's law enforcement fame is derived from two highly publicized captures involving locally infamous criminals. The first is an elusive fugitive with the fateful name of S. W. Lyman. The local papers reveled in the dramatic saga of Inspector Tichenor's twelve-mile pursuit of Lyman on horseback, eventually culminating with the inspector's leap from a moving train. Newspapers reported Lyman's reflections on the episode, "I'm rather sick, and I'm worn out. It's no fun being chased. I'm glad it's over."[16]

Tichenor's other highly publicized investigation consisted of the compilation of circumstantial evidence of the murderer of Nathan Wolff, the owner of a local pawnshop. The complexities of Tichenor's investigation against the dapper and confident suspect, Edward Martin, involved stakeouts, hunts for clothing, digging around under houses and "John Doe" warrants. When all was said and done, Tichenor and his fellow investigators were highly respected and deeply admired for bringing down such a shrewd "player."

During the trial, Martin made the mistake of approaching Tichenor in the hallway outside the courtroom. The exchange ended with an uncharacteristic flare of temper for the inspector as his thundering voice suppressed further exchanges from Martin. It is not known what was said, other than Tichenor's booming remark, "No, we haven't got the wrong man, Martin, and you know it!"[17]

Twentieth-Century Posses

Although it eventually took on a charitable flavor under Inspector Tichenor, Mayor Baker's call to arms through civilian power to enforce the law was not a new thing in the city of Portland. Posses, vigilant committees, and civil orders had always been a dynamic thread within the psyche of the settlers of the Oregon Territory and in the state that followed. In the new century, that tendency was further enabled by Section 192 of the 1903 charter granting the Portland City Council "power to appoint temporary policemen in times of emergency." [18] As an example of the posse tendency in the new century, in January 1918, a citizens' group concerned about the war effort met in Central Library Hall as a grass roots effort to assist the government in "reporting persons making seditious utterances." [19] Months later, in 1919 Governor Olcott lauded the American Legion's idea to organize a civilian reserve mobilized to eradicate anarchy and Bolshevism, pronouncing the effort to be ". . . the forerunner of similar efforts all over the country."[20] From the instantly deputized posse to the later-established committees mandated to ferret out sedition, Oregonians and Portlanders were characteristically ready to cluster into idealistic groups at the volunteer level.

Prepared to support his concerns for public safety, Mayor Baker understood that more affluent reservists were ripe for the picking among the local businessmen who had already been influenced by the postwar groundswell of volunteerism and home-based authority.[21] As a growing industrial town of youthful, entrepreneurial do-it-yourselfers, apparently Portland was particularly determined to protect what it had so recently gained in stature and establishment.

In January 1922, City Ordinance #40608 authorized the appointment of one hundred special policemen to serve in conjunction with the regular Police Department as part of an emergency declaration. Mayor Baker's "emergency" was a product of the correctly predicted elimination of the forty officers during a period of increased crime. On that same date, Inspector Tichenor was appointed head of the Vigilance Committee.

> *Section 1: That the Mayor be and he is hereby authorized to appoint one hundred persons of suitable character special policemen to act in conjunction with the police department of the City of Portland. . . .*
>
> *Section 2: Inasmuch as the ordinance is necessary for the immediate preservation of the public health, peace and safety of the City of Portland is*

Portland Police Vigilance Reserve Norman A. Thompson.
(Courtesy of Norman A. Thompson Jr.)

> *this: That in the annual budget for 1922 of the regular police department the number of regular policemen has been reduced and in the opinion of the Mayor and Council there is inadequate police protection being afforded the city . . . therefore an emergency is hereby declared. . . .*[22]

Immediately, reserve applications filled the police mailbox at city hall. By the end of the month, sixty-three men were appointed and given the oath of office as vigilance reserves.[23] After heading the committee by appointment until June 30, 1922, Inspector Carroll H. Tichenor was officially assigned to the task of commanding the new civilian police force.

Businessmen from both the east and the west side of the Willamette hoped to help the city with the loss of officers on the street due to budget cuts. Fueling the enthusiasm of the business community was the belief that the decision of the State Tax Commission was a product of a rural legislature out of touch with the needs of the state's largest city. Because law-enforcement needs in Portland were quite different than were those in many of the smaller towns of the state, the citizens of the metropolitan area rallied to cope with what was considered to be a poorly conceived state funding cut.

Norm A. Thompson

Along with several hundred local businessmen in a wave of applicants throughout the early to mid-1920s, local pipe shop owner and future sports outerwear clothier Norman A. Thompson applied to become a Portland Vigilance Police Officer under Mayor Baker. Upon reaching the application question requesting the reason why he wished to be appointed as a vigilance reserve, Thompson responded with the perfect penmanship that was later to become his trademark:

> *Because I wish to assist in any way possible the City of Portland. I make my living here, my home is here and I am willing to take my share of the responsibility.*[24]

His was a particularly eloquent explanation—one of many with a common theme safely preserved on hundreds of Portland vigilance reserve applications.[25]

Regardless of the motivations behind the formation of the Vigilance Reserves, the result was the creation of a camaraderie of successful citizens who were motivated to assist with the daily needs of the community.

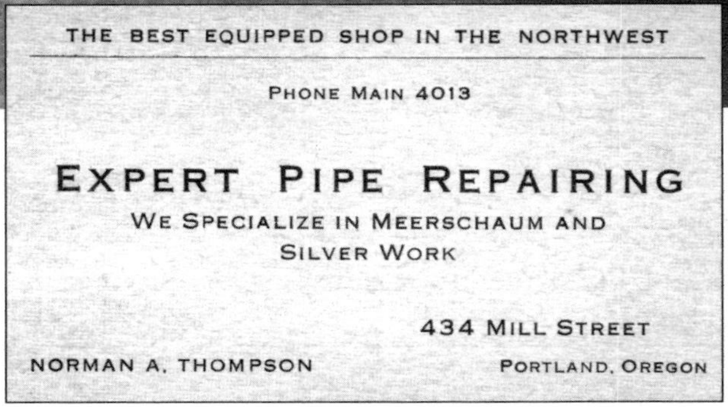

THE BEST EQUIPPED SHOP IN THE NORTHWEST

PHONE MAIN 4013

EXPERT PIPE REPAIRING

WE SPECIALIZE IN MEERSCHAUM AND SILVER WORK

434 MILL STREET

NORMAN A. THOMPSON

PORTLAND, OREGON

△ The pipe shop of Vigilance Reserve Sergeant Norman A. Thompson in downtown Portland, Oregon. (Courtesy of Norman A. Thompson Jr.)

▷ The business card of Norman A. Thompson. (Courtesy of Norman A. Thompson Jr.)

3

A MORE HUMAN AND HEARTBORN TASK

A common assumption is that the Portland Police Sunshine Division was established in 1923. As is the case for most things important enough to reconsider, historical investigation generally indicates that there is no specific moment of beginning for most institutions, but rather a series of events and persons that collectively symbolize an initiating moment in time. In actuality, 1923 represents the Christmas food basket campaign of the Portland Police Vigilance Reserves in its second year, with the food basket campaign of the uniformed police in its third year.

By 1922, police-sponsored food deliveries were no longer considered a one-time phenomenon—making it promising, but not permanent. Such pragmatism was quite normal in a developing "stumptown" unwilling to consider anything established unless it happened at least three times. Therefore, 1923 represented a year of parallel but separate Christmastime food deliveries made with practical, yet occasional, moments of cooperation between the uniformed police and the Portland Police Vigilance Reserves.

The Uniformed Police, 1922

On Christmas Eve 1922, the salaried, uniformed police delivered seventy food baskets to families in need of a special dinner for the holiday, more than doubling the gifts of the year before. The department paddy wagon "Black Maria" was used for most of the deliveries.[1] In an article titled, "Police Carry

Cheer to Poor Families," the *Oregonian* reported the distribution.

Into cheerful (service) for once in twelve months, the city's "Black Maria" was pressed yesterday and bluecoats whose supposed aim in life has been to enforce law and order, which is a cool part of the social brain, turned to a more human and heartborn task.

Seventy families in direst need, whom the world has somehow forgotten in the distribution of awards, are to be fed and generously fed, as the direct result of weeks of labor on the part of the individual members of the police bureau.

All day yesterday at the direction of Captain Circle, attaches of the bureau, men and women, worked putting up boxes and sacks of real food, chickens, roasts of beef, cabbages, apples, potatoes, sacks of flour and many other staples.

Portland merchants have contributed much of the food used. The rest has come from the contributions taken up from among the officers, who have seen at first hand the destitution that exists in many corners. The list passed through the central clearinghouse established by the public welfare bureau to prevent duplication. Visitors at the station yesterday were impressed by the size of the donations. The municipal courtroom and all its anterooms were packed with materials.

—*Oregonian,* Sunday, December 24, 1922[2]

Apparently, the department and community support of the 1921 Christmas food basket deliveries inspired more involvement the following year. Uniformed officers, bureau employees, and local merchants rallied to put together another year of food for those identified by police officers on the beat as in direst need.

The Vigilance Reserves, 1922

The following day, in what appears an enthusiastic echo, the *Oregonian*, edited by the mayor's good friend, Edgar Piper,[3] carried a similar article on an entirely different food delivery. It involved the newly

On Christmas Day 1922,
the Vigilance Reserves stand behind
Inspector Carroll Tichenor (front row left),
Chief Leon V. Jenkins (front row center),
and Mayor George Baker (front row right).
(Oregon Historical Society, #CN055599)

PORTLAND
VIGILANCE POLIC

founded Police Vigilance Reserves, the chief of police, the mayor, local merchants, and the delivery of two hundred Christmas food baskets.

With a great deal of fanfare and adjectives, a front-page article by C. H. Williams described with great sentimentality a tale of food baskets likened to the image of two hundred hearty, Christmas feasts, delivered, of course, with paramilitary precision by the civilian police force.

The lengthy article continued onto the second page, sporting a photograph of Mayor Baker, Chief Leon Jenkins, and Inspector Carroll Tichenor, flanked by the newly formed Portland Vigilance Reserves. At their feet are several food baskets brimming with generous quantities of pastries, meats, vegetables, fruits, toys, clothing, and items for the household. The vigilantes used their own cars, as owning a car was a requirement for service. Their deliveries ". . . covered the city from Linnton to Fulton and St. Johns to Lents."[4]

Apparently, with the good press of the 1921 Christmas basket deliveries of the regular uniformed police, the new civilian police reserves could not resist creating such an enchanting dynamic. Clearly, the Vigilance Reserves' first crusade to feed the poor was inspired by observing Captain Circle's model of the preceding years. Curiously, the mayor and the chief of police associated themselves in hearty support of the new effort with absolutely no mention or interest in the food deliveries that had been made by street officers the day before—or years before.

Regardless of who was first, a built-in reality prevailed. The reserves were local merchants and businessmen, and therefore had access to tremendous resources for the provisions within the baskets. The uniformed policemen had the heart for the task and a couple of personal automobiles as well as paddy wagons to aid in making deliveries, but they lacked the time, money, and personnel. The reserves had the flexibility, the resources, the contacts—and for their initiating year—the political interest of the mayor.

Parallel Efforts, 1923

In the following year, 1923, the tables turned and the vigilantes' food basket deliveries seemed to receive less attention, while the uniformed police food drive captured the imagination of the public. Nevertheless, vigilante reserves fervently gathered and stored food and sundries in the Routledge Seed and Floral Company warehouse until nine hundred baskets were delivered to 250 families under the leadership of Inspector Tichenor, Reserve Lieutenant B. C. Short, Reserve Sergeants J. C. Cain, O. H. Tracy, Virgil Cooper, Fred Grutze, Sam Dennison, U. D. Maxson, and H. L. DePenning.[5]

Included in the reserves' baskets this particularly cold winter were sixteen puppies donated by the Routledge firm to the first families willing to accept the fluffy embellishments. Their perseverance and generosity apart from the photo-opportunity conduct of city hall demonstrated that deeper intentions motivated the reserves than the political or professional benefits of publicity.

Although the reserves' effort was heroic, in 1923, the attention of the public rested on the uniformed police deliveries. Bringing that effort to the forefront was the misfortune of a particularly destitute family of seventeen persons. On December 23, an obscure story describing the overwhelming poverty of this family was printed deep in the *Oregonian* newspaper. In a page-nine article titled, "Two Families in Need, Men Seek Work of Any Kind, Aid Asked for 17 Grown People and Children by Members of Police Bureau," the cover-to-cover readers of the local paper tried to comprehend the circumstances of a struggling family.

If ever people needed the kind of offices of Santa Claus and the immediate help of neighbors, J. E. Hickson, wife and 11 children, and F. A. Hickson, wife and two children, destitute and living in one small damp tent near Seventy-ninth and Sandy, are those people.

Santa Claus may bring luxuries to many people, but these two families ask only the right to work and some decent place to live in until their fortunes improve. Their story is one of almost incredible hardship, but is vouched for by both the police department and the state game commission.

J. F. and F. A. Hickson, brothers, started from home in Montana with their families, to come to the coast where they heard work was plentiful. One is an auto mechanic and the other a laborer. One of J. F. Hickson's 11 children, a girl of 20 years began to show signs of incipient consumption and was advised by a doctor to move west. They sold out such small property as they had, got three cheap, second hand automobiles and began their journey. At Wenatchee, the mother of the brothers died and what money they had left went to pay for the funeral expenses.

> *When they crossed the Oregon line, near Arlington, J. F. Hickson saw two wild geese. This promised food, so he shot them to be immediately arrested by a game warden. . . . The judge at Arlington fined them $60 each. Without money, one of the machines* [cars] *was held.*
>
> *They arrived in Portland three days ago and got a tent at Seventy-ninth and Sandy, where they have lived since then, making no plea for help, but seeking any kind of work. When Patrolman Scott found them yesterday, they were reduced to less than $5. . . .*
>
> *"There must be someone in Portland who can afford to help these people." Said Sergeant Epps. "There must be someone who will come forward and lend a hand. We are waiting for that someone. Donations of food or money or offers of work, turned in through Captain Circle or myself will be taken out to those people immediately. Lets make it a merry Christmas for these people who have almost forgotten what happiness means."*
>
> —*Oregonian,* December 23, 1923[6]

After uniformed officers inspected the makeshift home, it was apparent that the needs of the family and the desperately ill daughter crowded in a soggy tent were beyond the capacity of the well-meaning police officers of Captain Circle's fund. The situation was discussed between officers and subsequently brought to the *Oregonian*. The hope was that the needs of the family might be expressed in the newspaper.

On December 24, the day following the rather small article on their plight, the front page reported an event symbolic of the three-way cooperation of the police, the *Oregonian* (also the owners of KGW Radio), and eventually the Vigilance Reserves. The article states that Santa Claus, in the guise of more than "two score Portlanders," found his way to the Hickson tent with donations of all kinds. Soon after the first article was printed, the telephones at the downtown police precinct began to ring continuously, making it necessary to man them with a full-time officer.

By day's end, patrolmen Rekdahl, Long, and Scott had moved all seventeen people into a house obtained by Mayor Baker and Captain Circle, and W. H. Embree offered jobs to the two brothers. In addition, six doctors offered their services to the twenty-year-old daughter, who was diagnosed that day with tuberculosis.[7]

An important piece in the events that led to mobilization of the public for the Hickson family was the few words in the plea for assistance that seem to remain central to police-sponsored charitable projects in Portland: "Their story is one of almost incredible hardship, but is vouched for by the police department and the state game warden."

With the truth of the family's story established by the police, the usual hesitations about generous giving were bypassed by a collective awareness that the police and the game warden, not generally known for their extensive compassion, would only report the situation to such lengths if it were dire.

With the unifying help of the publicity of the *Oregonian* through the police, the needs of the poor transcended hesitant associations, previous political stumping, or the resistance to combine resources. The vigilance reserves worked steadfastly on their food drive; the uniformed police did the same on theirs—with the Hicksons' situation thrown in the mix. The common denominator was that the situation for many families, especially the Hicksons', was desperate.

In the midst of the local depression, Mayor Baker did not have to try to appear concerned for political purposes—he truly was concerned. The house that he quietly located for the Hickson family was one in a long line of subterranean gestures throughout his carrier that substantiated another assessment of his character made by historian E. Kimbark MacColl.

> *These were not contrived events, although George Baker loved to put on a good act. . . . George Baker was an emotional gregarious man who loved people and loved his country more. America had been good to George and such acts of generosity were a means of expressing his appreciation.*[8]

Late into the night on Christmas Eve 1923, Captain Circle and the uniformed day relief of the Portland Police Department delivered the second half of the now 266 food deliveries at the end of their shifts. Several hundred merchants contributed to the baskets, and the men and women employed by the police department did the packing, with the help of a few good-natured reserves.

The need to compile the provisions and deliver them off duty became important due to the fact that the sheer volume would interrupt police services. For Captain Circle, the idea of offering food to the poor from the hands of police was expanding beyond the capacity of the small wooden box on his desk. The Police Department needed to consider a more effective way to manage its concern for the poor.

In the midst of the flurry of Christmas Eve deliveries, a reporter asked how the officers got down the chimney to deliver the baskets. Captain Circle declared, "Just like Christmas trees grow inside homes in the living room corner overnight."[9]

Twenty-eight years later, knowing that Captain Circle was its unofficial founder, Mayor Dorothy McCullough Lee[10] appointed him commander of the well-established product of his efforts, by then known as the Portland Police Sunshine Division.

4

OWLS, GOATS, DIGNITARIES, AND SUCH MATTER

A recap of KGW Radio's Keep Growing Wiser Order of the Hoot Owls' first performance for the Portland listening audience is found in KGW's radio-broadcast column in the *Sunday Oregonian* of January 30, 1923. Readers lucky enough to own a crystal set could recapture the fun and frolic of the Friday evening show.

Broadcasting from KGW

> *The KGW (Keep Growing Wiser) Order of the Hoot Owls started into action in the padded cell in the* Oregonian *tower last night with an awful flutter. Promptly at 11:00 o'clock the Grand Eagle owl, Charles F. Berg flew in, followed by Mayor George L. Baker, J. W. Hofmann and other exalted Ignavi. They had scarcely roosted on the imperial perch when the Manila string sextet, made up of players on all kinds of string instruments, and Larry Franklin, the man that can make a piano talk, also lit on a nearby perch, and the fun started.*
>
> *Owing to the important business of getting the Hoot Owls off on the right wing, only those members who were in the studio were initiated. So many applications for membership had been received that it was impossible to consider them all at the first meeting. The applications have been numbered as they were received and initiation will be given in the same order.*
>
> *Details of the initiation ceremonies were withheld from the press, and reporters were not*

allowed in the padded cell. Special correspondents lined the corridors outside, but could hear only the muffled sounds, which seeped through the heavily padded walls when the revelry was highest. Reports were that the loudest noises which escaped were those incidental to Mayor Baker's ride on the goat. Charlie Berg led the animal and the exalted Ignavi wielded the big sticks. . . .

—*Oregonian,* Tuesday January 30, 1923[1]

On January 3, 1922, nearly one year before the Exalted Ignavi of the Royal Order of the Hoot Owls offered their first goat ride, the National Radio Service Bulletin announced an amendment to Radio Laws and Regulations of the United States defining what would be defined as the Class 2 broadcast. It read as follows,

Class 2: Licenses of this class are required for all transmitting radio stations used for broadcasting news, concert, lectures, and such matter.[2]

If one takes the time to review the memorabilia and hear descriptions of the Hoot Owls radio broadcast format, it is evident that the "KGW Royal Order of the Hoot Owls," as one of the nation's first variety shows, qualified as "such matter." The importance of "such matter" to the history of the Sunshine Division is familiar knowledge to persons who waited beside the crystal set for these familiar words:

When we gather for the meeting
and they put us on the air,
We will send a friendly greeting
to the people everywhere,
So accept our invitation,
hear each merry jest we bring,
Turn your dials and get the station
and listen while we sing:
Hello, Everybody, here we are again,
Growing Wiser Hoot Owls, Friday half-past ten,
Everybody's happy, no use feeling blue,
So Hoot, Hoot, Hoot Owls, Hoot, from KGW.

The Hungari

On December 26, 1924, nearly two years into the show, a banquet called the "Hungari" offered good food and three hours of entertainment for its lucky ticket holders. The gathering was to commemorate the second year of the phenomenally popular "Keep Growing Wiser Royal Order of the Hoot Owls" radio program. The first speaker was Edgar B. Piper, editor of the *Oregonian,* and therefore the founder of the newly established KGW radio station. His speech reflected upon his reasons for bringing the light-hearted program into existence.

> *The Hoot Owls were organized to spread sunshine at midnight. It was the plan to spread more brightness and light into some lives that otherwise might be darkened. It was too, to disseminate further the always needed spirit of good will.*[3]

Piper's greatest challenge throughout his speech was the background antics of the Hoot Owl Degree Team as they took advantage of the opportunity to be seen, not just heard, leaving the crowd completely inattentive to his words.

The second speaker was Bishop Walter Sumner, who, between the *Maa's* of Sweet William (the goat whose sole purpose was to initiate new members to the Order via a rollicking goat-ride) explained that behind the Hoot Owls' jollity was a note of service to those shut in their own homes who could not form the usual contacts with their fellows.

The final speaker, Mayor Baker, thanked the *Oregonian* and therefore KGW for its expansive broadcasts that literally put Portland on the map to a listening audience up to six thousand miles away.

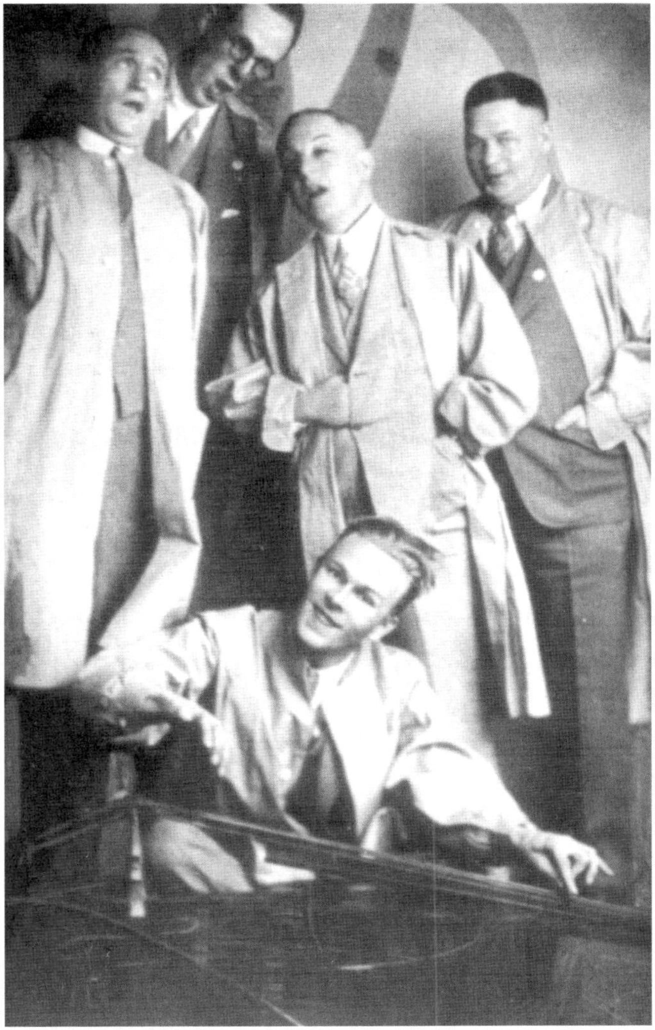

Five of the many "KGW (Keep Growing Wiser) Royal Order of the Hoot Owls" offer jollity for the camera. Center left with glasses stands Harry Grannatt, and leaning into him from the center is Charles F. Berg. (City of Portland, SPARC, SSD Slide Collection, A2002-009)

Good Citizenship

The Hoot Owls telecast maintained a wide appeal to older children as well as adults. It managed to maintain the balance of adult-oriented humor within its effort to encourage good citizenship in the young and the not-so-young.

For children allowed to stay up until 11:00 P.M. on Friday nights, the show took a satirical approach to familiar fables—communicating the original values of the well-known story while offering a certain twist. In Volume One of *Hoot Owl Classics*, a book published in 1928 by the Rainbow Division of the Hoot Owl Order, listeners could savor their favorite "revised" skits at any time. On one episode of the weekly telecast, Dean Collins offered his version of the story of the "Goose That Laid the Golden Egg" later to be published in the *Hoot Owl Classics*.

> *Tonight, dear children, I want to tell you a brand new model of the story of the Goose That Laid the Golden Egg.*
>
> *Once upon a time, there was a humble farmer and his wife. They had a farm, four mortgages, a broken-down binder and wagon with two chattel mortgages, a house, a barn, two horses, four cows, a gosling, 23 dogs, a squirrel rifle and a son with a hook worm . . .*
>
> *. . . And they all lived happily ever after, and refinanced the golden egg-laying goose eight times, and found that it paid better than the mortgages on the farm, for the purchasers of the stock were the only ones who had to foot any bills. And the moral of the story dear children is: Love will find a way.*[4]

Upon reading the surprisingly sophisticated local humor of the *Hoot Owl Classics* Volumes One and Two by Dean Collins and Harry Grannatt, one might wonder if the children of the 1920s and 1930s understood the stories at all. When asked, the listeners remaining to reminisce about the show generally say, "What I remember is how much we laughed. And how much we thought we could do to help someone else."[5] The youngsters were allowed to stay up late with their families, but most importantly, they could experience an irreverent, laugh-till-you-cry humor with their parents—with a moral to the story.

What kept everyone tuning in was the irreverent appeal. Through the Hoot Owls, important businessmen and leaders in the community demonstrated their more earthy characteristics

while participating in a variety show that demonstrated their genuine concern for the community. Mockingly, the "Degree Team" adopted fictional titles directed clearly at excessive behavior and inflated self-importance. It appears to be no accident that the names of the Owls are a direct and disrespectful blow, making silly the intimidating hierarchical titles of extremely serious organizations such as the Ku Klux Klan.

In the early 1920s, the Klan was on the rise with its second of three phases of activity in the United States. Until 1924, the Klan's superpatriotic theme in post–World War I Oregon was rather effective in its attempt to pull in local business and political figures of the city of Portland and the state of Oregon. After its rapid, two-year climb in popularity in Oregon, based primarily upon its pro-American and anti-Catholic agenda, the even more extreme and completely racial agenda of the Klan was gradually exposed. Its organizational influence would dissipate as fast as it began, leaving a wake of personal destruction. With the tables turning, persons in leadership and business were quick to attack

Volume One Hoot Owl Classics *printed by the Rainbow Division of the KGW Hoot Owls Broadcast. (City of Portland, SPARC, SSD Collection, A2002-009)*

Hoot Owls Opener

(Tune: Funicula Funicula)

— 1 —

SOLO: *Oh look!*
The hands around the clock go scooting
To half past ten!

CHORUS: *It's half past ten!*

SOLO: *Once more*
It's time the Hoot Owls started hooting .
They're here again.

CHORUS: *We're here again.*

SOLO: *Tune in!*
Tune in and give yourselves an earful
That's bound to suit.

CHORUS: *We try to suit.*

SOLO: *From now to midnight, let us all be cheerful*
The Hoot Owls Hoot.

GENERAL CHORUS:
Hoot Owls! Hoot Owls!
Here we are again!
Hoot Owls! Hoot Owls!
Friday . . . half past ten
To hoo, to hoo
To hoo, to hoo
To hoo, to hoo
To hoo, to hoo
Hi-falutin' . . . hootin' . . . tootin'
Hoot Owls here again.

— 2 —

SOLO: *We're here*
To get a jolly exclamation
Right off our chest

CHORUS: *Right off our chest.*

SOLO: *And KGW, our own home station*
We like it best

CHORUS: *We like it best.*

SOLO: *Tonight, from off the old home roost*
To bring you mirth [*a-starting*

CHORUS: *To bring you mirth.*

SOLO: *Our flight upon the air is now departing*
Above the earth

CHORUS: *For all we're worth.*

GENERAL CHORUS:
Hoot Owls! Hoot Owls! etc., etc.

Pandora

ONCE upon a time, dear children, there lived a couple of young men by the names of Prometheus and Epimetheus, respectively.

If you have kept up in your reading, you will know that Prometheus means forethought and Epimetheus means afterthought. The names were given according to the line that the two young men shined best in.

Prometheus always carried fire, theft, accident, collision, liability and other insurance on his car, his house, his life and anything else he happened to have lying around. He never let a Saturday forenoon go by without taking his little clock down to the savings bank and letting the cashier unlock it and take out the dimes he had put in to keep it running. And he always kept his umbrella and goloshes handy by the door in case he should wish to go out at any time.

Epimetheus was just the opposite. He could lead you over town and point out any number of business sites and say: "I remember when I could have got that for a good ax handle and a plug of tobacco. I sure would be on easy street now if I had made that trade." He never knew where his umbrella was, and he'd give his last quarter to a panhandler any time without a thought as to where he was going to get the rent for the landlady.

Well, the gods of ancient Greece, in due

Volume One *Hoot Owl Classics* printed by
the Rainbow Division of the KGW Hoot Owls Broadcast.
(City of Portland, SPARC, SSD Collection, A2002-009)

extreme fraternal orders and organizations. Enter the Hoot Owls.

The Hoot Owls appear to be taunting the secrecy and organizational structure of extreme fraternal organizations with a catch-me-if-you-can reversal filled with humor and rhetoric. The Hoot Owls irreverently adopted their own royal titles. Names such as "The Grand Screech" (Charles F. Berg, Proprietor), "The Grand Scream" (Frank Sardam, Insurance), "The Grand Schmoos" (Barnett H. Goldstein, Lawyer), "The Grand Stringbean" (Harry Grannatt, Insurance Engineer, Dooly & Co.), "The Grand Sketch" (Edward S. Reynolds, Cartoonist, *Oregonian),* "The Grand Sermon" (Walter Taylor Sumner, Bishop of Oregon), "The Grand Sonnet" (Dean Collins, Feature Writer, *Oregonian),* "The Grand Skipano" (William Robinson Boone, Organist and Musical Director), and "The Grand Serenader" (Charles R. Whitehead, Musical Director, Dufwin Theatre).[6]

Such titles were playfully thrown about the broadcast with dramatic and overzealous piety. The tongue-in-cheek humor made a playful mockery of the seriousness of secret organizations presenting them as silly—even though they were a significant and thriving element in many social circles.

Most of all, Hoot Owl humor was welcome at a time when Portlanders were heavily burdened with postwar fear and concern for the volatility of the world and the vulnerability of the local economy. In response, people throughout the region tuned in by the thousands to hear the group of renegade businessmen bent on knocking the pegs from under those who needed to "lighten up."

The adult appeal also had much to do with the persons who were the initial members of the Hoot Owls. The broadcast lineup involved a collection of successful local businessmen from around town, as well as a few specialists to offer voice and musical instrumentation.

Mel Blanc

Although not an early member, an important and beloved character-voice performer and musician was Melvin Blanc. As a performer in the South Parkway Minstrel Show of the South Parkway Club of Portland, and eventually of Bugs Bunny and Porky Pig fame, Melvin Blanc, "Juvenile Singer," was a guest of the Owls on March 2, 1924, at the age of fifteen. He performed two of the numbers he was to perform at the Commercial High School Vaudeville Show at the Lincoln High School Auditorium. His voice was exceptional, but the performance was not characteristic of the role he would play in the future.

Foreshadowing what was to come was effectively demonstrated by the day-to-day experience of Norm Thompson Jr., son of the pipe shop owner and clothier, who shared work duties with young Melvin Blanc in Norm Thompson Sr.'s pipe shop. Norm Thompson Jr. recalls, "Mel was a stock boy in my dad's pipe shop. He used to grab a cigar and do that Bunny thing all the time. . . ."[7]

After his second appearance on the show, Blanc would become the "Grand Snicker" and the youngest Hoot Owl of the broadcast, having been hired immediately out of Portland's Lincoln High School for twenty-five dollars a week. Later Blanc stated in his autobiography:

It was KGW that gave me my start in Radio, soon after Lincoln High School and I parted company with mutual sighs of relief in 1927. Apparently word of my abilities as a story teller, musician and vocalist reached the station, which was headquartered in the Oregonian *Building at Alder Street and Sixth Avenue. Someone phoned in programming and asked me to sing on a Friday evening program called the Hoot Owls.*

"Sure, I'd love to. Which song?"

"Juanita," I was told, a beautiful traditional Spanish ballad. What splendid luck; I knew its enchanting melody and lyrics by heart: 'Soft o'er the fountain, lingering falls the southern moon . . .' However, it turned out the station had a different "Juanita" in mind.[8]

With his friends, family, and peers from the South Parkway Minstrel Show, a thriving and diverse collection of Portland's greatest homegrown Jewish and multicultural talent listening on, Melvin whimpered a satirical Hoot Owl rewrite of "Juanita" that would establish him forever as a member of the Royal Order.

I'd be a wreck when I got the check,
I prayed that she'd get indigestion.
But such luck, it was out of the question.
They say nanny goats can eat soda cans
and such,
My girl eats things nanny goats won't touch.
I call her my sweet Wanita:
"Wanna eat, wanna eat," Wanita.

The Hoot Owls, soon to be taken away from the *Oregonian* building in Black Maria, the patrol wagon named to affirm its ominous resemblance to a hearse. Left to right outside the wagon is Lt. C. H. Tichenor, Charles F. Berg, Dean Collins, Harry Grannatt, and Attorney John Logan as the Hoot Owls' legal advocate. Inside the wagon are Harry F. Anderson of NBC, Tige Reynolds, and C. O. Chatterton. (City of Portland, SPARC, SSD Collection, A2000-026.43)

SEASON'S
GREETINGS

Blanc goes on to say:

It was an immediate hit with both the audience and the cast, which I was asked to join on a steady basis. The salary? A pittance. But I eagerly accepted, for the "Hoot Owls," a charity show presided over by local businessmen, was a city-wide favorite. Needy citizens would call in, and the Portland Police Department's Sunshine Division would deliver a free food package to their front door. In addition to serving a worthy cause, "The Hoot Owls" was damn entertaining. None of the cast was a show business professional, but each could have held his own with some of the comedy writers and performers I would later encounter in Hollywood. Our little radio troupe was called the Degree Team, and all members were accorded descriptive appellations: My friend Harry Grannatt, an insurance salesman, was nearly seven feet tall; hence his sobriquet "The Grand Stringbean." Charles Berg, who ran a downtown department store, was the "Grand Screecher." A local preacher was, naturally, "The Grand Sermon." Because of my faculty for fetching laughs, I became "The Grand Snicker."[9]

~

Harry Grannatt (center) with Officer George Hempe and Ted Baum, as Grannatt hangs a wreath as only his seven-foot-tall frame could. (City of Portland, SPARC, SSD Collection, A2002-009)

Proprietor Charles F. Berg of the fashionable Charles F. Berg Department Store that brought East-Coast apparel and art-deco architectural curves to downtown Portland held the title of "The Grand Screech." Insurance executive Frank Sardam expressed himself as "The Grand Scream." The creative genius behind the fast-moving script and satirical compositions was the cooperative effort of Dean Collins (The Grand Sonnett), a feature writer for the *Portland Telegram* and Harry Grannatt (The Grand Stringbean), who solemnly declared himself an "Insurance Engineer" for Dooly & Co.

Every Wednesday the frustrated/talented, entrepreneur/performers would meet at the Benson Hotel, read the paper for current events, eat lunch, and rough out the script for the Friday evening show. For the year 1923, the Hoot Owl format rested upon satirical fun, local musical talent, and creative genius. In 1924, the Hungari heralded the show's evident transition into cooperating with the philanthropical efforts of the Police Department, the Vigilance Reserves, the business community, and the listening city to bring "Sunshine" to those in need.

Mel Blanc, Harry Grannatt, and Dean Collins
reminiscing over Hoot Owl memorabilia.
(City of Portland, SPARC, SSD Collection, A2002-009)

5

THE SUNSHINE FUND

In a 1975 letter to Isabell Hoyt, past chairman of the Sunshine Board of Directors Ray Carr[1] reminisced about the beginnings of the Sunshine Division.

> *To go back . . . the very beginning of Sunshine Division was started when the radio station, KGW, with Dick Haller chief announcer, (later to Honolulu station for many years) . . . developed a format called "Keep Growing Wiser" Order of the Hoot Owls that puts on a program 11 to 12 midnight every Friday night . . . with a certain amount of horse-play, music, entertainment . . . with an initiation of some prominent citizen into the order. Barry Goldstein (Judge-Attorney) usually conducted the obligation . . . Dean Collins,* News Telegram *columnist/poet had an original poem . . . usually with a line about "dill pickles coming rolling in from the sea. . . .*[2]

On December 12, 1924, the beginning of the second Christmas season of the KGW Hoot Owls, three seasonal projects were announced. The first was the Sunshine Fund to be collected in order to spread sunshine among the needy at Christmastime. The next was a drive (a seasonal extension of the Rainbow Division) for crystal sets to be given as Christmas presents to isolated "shut-ins and invalids." The third was an announcement of the aforementioned event called the Hoot Owl Hungari, which was a banquet in celebration of the second anniversary of the organization.

Henry W. Metzger's Friday night airtime announcement of the need for contributions for the Christmas Fund and the crystal sets more than doubled, in one night, the sporadic contributions of the previous two years.

The Grand Sermon

Ordinarily, the Hoot Owl broadcast was divided into a variety of time slots called "Divisions." The Rainbow Division segment, offered by Bishop Walter Sumner (The Grand Sermon), was the portion of the show that was the first charitable expression of the Hoot Owls beyond their general concern for the development of fun-loving young citizens. The creative, ahead-of-their-time imaginations involved in the program assumed that shut-ins would benefit greatly from the social contact of listening to live radio broadcasts. Thus began Sumner's occasional on-the-air pleas for listeners to notify the station of persons unable to purchase a radio. As a symbol of traveling through the air, the title "Rainbow Division" expressed the bridge created by the transmission of radio waves from the KGW Tower to persons listening in their homes.

Bishop Walter Taylor Sumner

As the broadcasts progressed throughout 1923, the Hoot Owls, with Bishop Sumner as their prominent spokesman, became recognized as a charitable voice available to inform the community of special needs—beyond radios. In an interview in 1971 with the *Oregon Journal,* Harry S. Grannatt, also known as the Grand Stringbean, expressed the new discovery of the profound influence of early radio on public awareness in this way, "Once we asked for a wheel chair and we got eight."[3]

Bishop Walter Taylor Sumner, D.D., the most eloquent "Owl," was better known as the Grand Sermon. He was also known as the Forth Episcopal Bishop of the Oregon Diocese, one of the most influential religious positions in Oregon. Bishop Sumner was a quietly educated man who years later, upon his death, surprised his admirers with his credentials. And, after applying to be a Portland Police Vigilance Reserve in 1923, the Bishop was appointed by Inspector Tichenor to be the Portland Police Vigilance Reserve Chaplain.

As a Dartmouth graduate (1898) with a bachelor in science, and the recipient of several honorary degrees, as well as a doctorate in divinity from the Western Seminary in Chicago, Sumner was responsible for the creation of what would become the "Sunshine Fund" portion of the Hoot Owls' radio show.

The terms "Division," "Fund," and "Department" seem to be used interchangeably throughout the early documents and articles describing the show, but the Sunshine Fund segment emerged from the need to separate the Rainbow Division from other community-oriented activities. Originally, the "Sunshine Fund," coined from the phrase, ". . . to bring a little sunshine into their lives," appears to be an attempt to bring joy and "light" into the lives of those with physical, day-to-day needs. The Rainbow Division appears to have been the segment of the show designed to solicit the names of persons specifically needing a crystal radio set to socially connect them to the world outside their homes. Both divisions continued throughout the life of the broadcast. Both divisions became official by name on Friday, December 12, 1924, at least as far as the Hoot Owls' involvement is concerned.

Originally, pre-Sunshine Fund, radio announcements asked the listening audience for items such as wooden legs, firewood, food, or fuel with the nature of the requests driven by the individual circumstances. In addition, there were appeals for public attendance at community gatherings for charitable causes. For practical reasons, the Grand Sermon maintained an important distinction between the two divisions of the show. It took a concerted effort of radio salesmen, technicians, donors, and volunteers to put a crystal set in a home. The home required effective electrical outlets, and often the older donated sets required headphones. Much like the technologies of any era, people needed to be shown how to use the sets. Training on maintenance, how to find the stations, and then to control volume and tone were necessary elements in donating the new technology to an inexperienced listener. The Rainbow Division was maintained by an entirely different group of volunteers than was the Sunshine Division.

With Sumner as chaplain for the Portland Police Vigilance Reserves, the Sunshine Fund mirrored the organizational characteristics and affiliations of Bishop Sumner. Under his guidance and concern, the growth of the Fund mandated an announcement that it would be audited annually, and would focus upon the emerging physical needs of persons in the community.

With the effective administration of the charitable energies of the Portland Police Bureau through Inspector Tichenor, the pleas for public donations through Bishop Sumner of the Hoot Owls, and the unabashed support of the business community, the entity known as the Sunshine Fund exploded with activity. The greatest challenge of the embryonic organization eventually named in a 1926 auditor's report "The Sunshine Fund of the Police Department, the 'Hoot Owls' and Police Reserve, and the City of Portland" was whether or not it had the capacity to meet demands. Not the demands of the poor and hungry, but rather the capacity to accommodate the demands of dealing with massive donations and volunteerism in addition to the needs of the hungry.

Although active in 1923, the name Captain Harry Circle no longer is found in newspaper accounts of the next several Christmas seasons. It appears that the duty to oversee the charitable efforts of the Police Bureau was assigned to the Vigilance Reserves under Inspector Tichenor. Time and resources would dictate that the reserves bear the responsibility of the activities with sworn officers participating at will. In this way, the officers could locate families in need and offer support when they had the time, leaving the primary role of the organization of the fast-growing Fund to those who had the time and resources.

It is apparent that Captain Circle understood the necessity to allow his idea to flourish in the best possible environment. His administrative responsibilities at Central Precinct occupied too much of his career to take on more. It was a natural transition to allow someone with an indisputably familiar face—that of Inspector Tichenor—the chance to refine the process. Years later, many of Circle's greatest admirers did not realize that he had established the original donation processes for what would become the Sunshine Division. With no record of complaint on his part, he seemed content to know that things would move on without him.

Under Tichenor and Sumner, the 1924 Christmas food drive was extremely successful. The following is an excerpt from the *Oregonian*, Christmas Day 1924:

> *. . . An appeal for the needy had been broadcast by the Owls through KGW in the course of their weekly programs for the last week or so. Response of the radio listeners was spontaneous and liberal. The money as received was turned over to Henry W. Metzger, Grand Slam of the Hoot Owls organization, who in turn slipped it to the police department to purchase Christmas joy for those who otherwise would have been without it.*

Members of the police department were no less zealous in making personal contributions and in soliciting generous donations for the same purpose.

The result was that yesterday morning tons of foodstuffs had been accumulated at the municipal garage at Fourth and Market streets when vigilantes appeared with their own cars prepared to undertake the distribution of the baskets, prepared in advance.

The packing of the baskets represented several nights work on the part of the vigilantes and uniformed members of the police department, off duty . . .

. . . Regular police force members also who have given of their time and money in preparation for the task of caring for the needy of Portland during the holidays assisted further in the work.[4]

Duplication and Accountability

Important to the citizenry and city hall was the issue of duplication. With two police-related organizations, sworn and reserves, citizens were confused at times. And with clearing house lists available to both organizations to avoid duplication, the question became: Why not share the same list of persons already receiving aid produced by the Welfare Bureau, and why not combine donations to create more-complete baskets? Also important to the citizenry was the issue alluded to through the previous editorial comment, ". . . The money as received was turned over to Henry W. Metzger, Grand Slam of the Hoot Owls organization, who in turn *slipped* it to the police department to purchase Christmas joy. . . ." During the period of Prohibition and postwar uneasiness, the public justifiably maintained a growing concern for corruption within the Police Bureau. National Prohibition came at a time when America entered one of the most socially innovative eras in its history. The inevitable result was widespread violation of the liquor law, with the crux of the problem the impossibility of enforcing it.[5] For that Christmas Day, the editor's playful choice of words exposed a constructive use of private money rather than a corrupt one.

Before and including 1924, the municipal garage and the police headquarters were the temporary home of Christmas dinners for thousands of people, beginning the end of November. The logistics were difficult at best. It was becoming apparent that a headquarters away from the downtown precinct was in order so municipal activities could continue uninterrupted.

The following year, in the building formerly occupied by Jones's Cash Store at East Second and Belmont, the Vigilance Reserves, the Hoot Owls, and the sworn uniformed police set up shop on December 1, 1925. The three entities would distribute food baskets and assist the needy for the holiday season. Inspector Tichenor remained at the "Headquarters" for the entire month, supervising the work and receiving and sorting donations.[6] Ordinarily, his desk was located at the headquarters of the Vigilance Reserves on Seventh and Alder, the second floor of what was then East Precinct.

To account for the tremendous input and output of the Division, the Police Bureau asked Sawtell, Withington & Company, Accountants and Auditors, located in the Chamber of Commerce building, to perform annual audits of the Sunshine Fund. The concern was to protect Captain Tichenor and his assistants from being accused of incongruities.

In Tichenor's handwritten ledger book, one will find meticulous records of every transaction.[7] His concern for detail was a welcome administrative skill, as well as an important element to demonstrate high accountability within the fund-raising efforts. His challenge was that listeners of the Hoot Owls broadcast would hear of the needs of individuals as reported by reserves to Bishop Sumner, then meet the performers at the door of the radio station after the evening broadcast to offer their donations. Small crowds of sleepy-eyed donors often stood for hours waiting at the base of the KGW Tower for the Hoot Owls to emerge. Held in their arms were groceries, crutches, blankets or any number of items; in their hands—envelopes of cash. Many times, reluctant Hoot Owls would go home from the KGW lobby with pockets full of cash intended for the Sunshine Fund, not quite sure what else to do with the contributions at 12:30 in the morning.

With Tichenor in place, and no precedence-setting model to imitate, his flexible methodology began as determined by the enthusiasm, perspectives, and talents of the extreme variety of persons involved. His only guide was his knack for positive human interaction amid the quagmire of the political and social complexities of the twenties. The ability to effectively deal with those complexities quite possibly explains the Sunshine Division's organizational resilience regardless of more than eighty years of political and economic pressures. The cross-section of people, businesses, and organizations with which Tichenor dealt is mind-boggling. Some reserves were lawyers and accountants; some were small business owners and shopkeepers; some were butchers and grocers. And Tichenor's capacity to pull people in created a resource base that literally filled his shelves.

▽ Vigilance Police data card for Victor Welsh, a reserve offering grocery and butchering skills to the collective capabilities of the volunteer police force of Portland as well as his supplemental police activities. This was one of hundreds of cards kept by Inspector Tichenor along with Vigilance Police applications and photographs. (City of Portland, SPARC, SSD Collection, A2002-026)

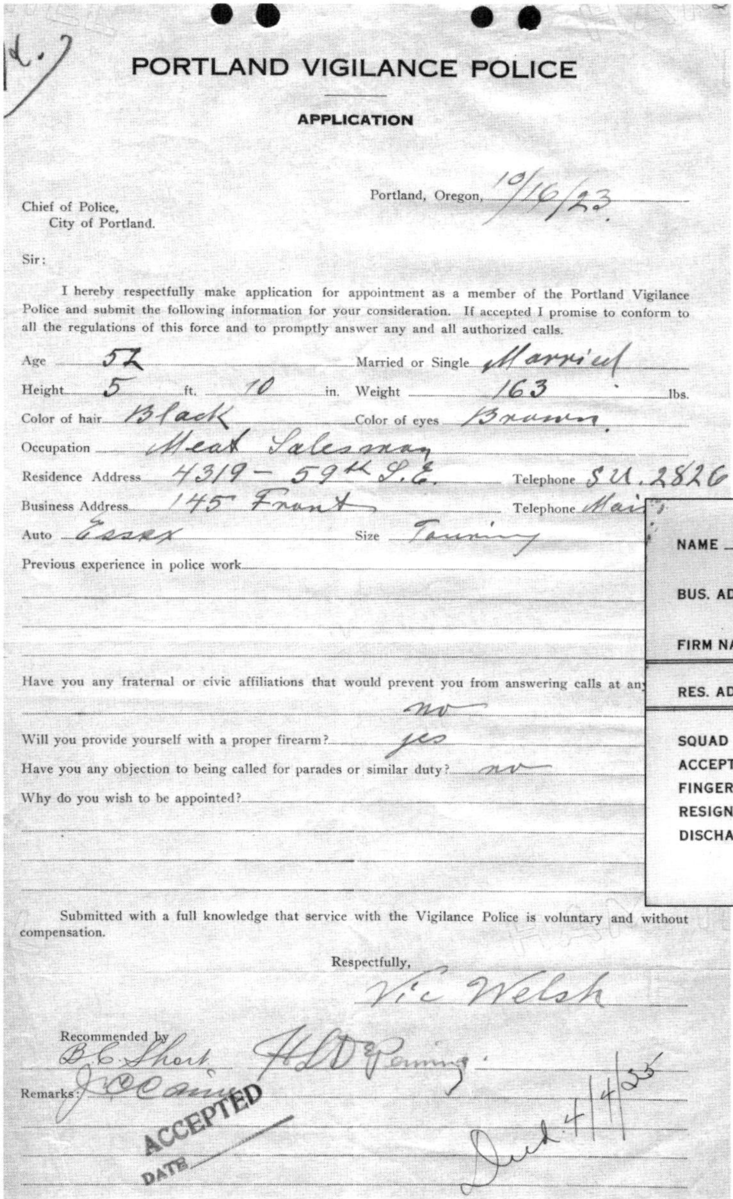

PORTLAND VIGILANCE POLICE

APPLICATION

Portland, Oregon, 10/16/23.

Chief of Police,
City of Portland.

Sir:

I hereby respectfully make application for appointment as a member of the Portland Vigilance Police and submit the following information for your consideration. If accepted I promise to conform to all the regulations of this force and to promptly answer any and all authorized calls.

Age 52 Married or Single Married

Height 5 ft. 10 in. Weight 163 lbs.

Color of hair Black Color of eyes Brown

Occupation Meat Salesman

Residence Address 4319 – 59th S.E. Telephone SU. 2826

Business Address 145 Front Telephone Mai[n]

Auto Essex Size Touring

Previous experience in police work

Have you any fraternal or civic affiliations that would prevent you from answering calls at any [time]? no

Will you provide yourself with a proper firearm? yes

Have you any objection to being called for parades or similar duty? no

Why do you wish to be appointed?

Submitted with a full knowledge that service with the Vigilance Police is voluntary and without compensation.

Respectfully,
Vic Welsh

Recommended by
B. C. Short H. L. DePoning

Remarks: J. O. Canne

ACCEPTED
DATE

Died 4/4/25

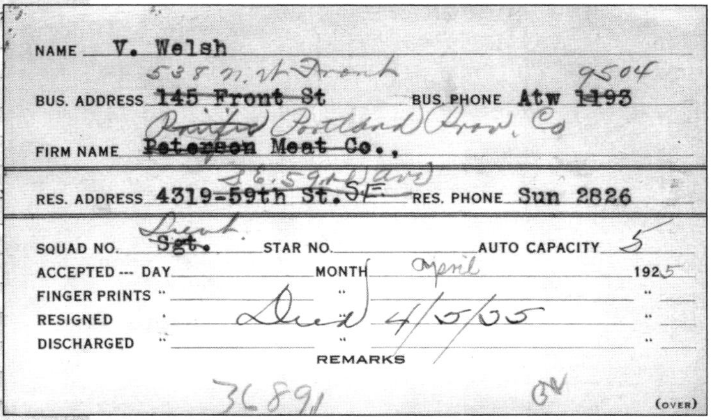

NAME V. Welsh

538 N. W. Front

BUS. ADDRESS ~~145 Front St~~ BUS. PHONE Atw ~~1193~~ 9504

~~[illegible]~~ Portland Prov. Co

FIRM NAME ~~Peterson Meat Co.~~

56.59th (Ave)

RES. ADDRESS ~~4319-59th St. SE~~ RES. PHONE Sun 2826

Lieut.

SQUAD NO. ~~Sgt.~~ STAR NO. AUTO CAPACITY 5

ACCEPTED --- DAY MONTH April 1925

FINGER PRINTS " " "

RESIGNED " Died 4/5/25 "

DISCHARGED " " "

REMARKS

36891

(OVER)

◁ Vigilance Police application for Vic Welsh. (City of Portland, SPARC, SSD Collection, A2002-026)

Sergeant Vic Welsh, Portland Vigilance Police.
(City of Portland, SPARC, SSD Collection, A2002-026)

One example of a person inspired to help was Vic Welsh, who signed on with the reserves in October 1923, later to rise to the rank of lieutenant. As a meat salesman and grocer, he and many others were instrumental in establishing the long-term working relationship between the Sunshine Division and the local Meat Cutters unions. Every Christmas, due to coordinated efforts between the unions and the Division, plenty of good cuts always filled the Christmas baskets.

It was speculated by many in the city of Portland that Inspector Tichenor's inexhaustible concern for the poor was a product of his own poverty-stricken childhood.

> *The hard conditions of poverty are not theoretical to Captain Tichenor* [later promoted], *but very real. He was born at Port Orford, Oregon, and at an early age his father died, leaving a large family with very little means wherewith to carry on. Being next to the eldest, he helped to shoulder the burden, and hustled and worked diligently to aid in the support of the family. . . . This deeply personal and intimate experience with the realities of life under difficult conditions explains Captain Tichenor's instant understanding and sympathy with the problems of those in need. His heart is in his work, for he knows what destitution means.*[8]

During his time as commander, from 1922 to his death in 1942, Tichenor established an administrative system that effectively recognized a three-element infrastructure to facilitate the grass-roots outpouring of law enforcement–based charitable energy toward the poor. What past–Sunshine Division Board Member Gerry Frank now calls "the genius of the Sunshine Division"[9] consisted of the administrative support of the three-way dynamics between law enforcement, merchant cooperation, and advertising.

Intuitively, Tichenor seemed to know what time has since substantiated. The tenacity of the Sunshine Division depended equally upon the three-way dynamics of the image of the compassionate police officer linked to the entrepreneurial generosity of the local merchant and articulated by cost-free publicity.

More importantly, Tichenor understood that there were thousands of struggling people in his community in need of emergency food relief. As the commander of the Reserves, and therefore custodian of their charitable works, he became the organizational founder of an unorthodox, self-sustaining charitable mechanism in a peculiar position to do something about local hunger.

Ten steers surrounded by members of the Meat Cutters Union who offered their carving skills in 1926. Volunteers include William Hogan, Earnest Bennett, Ed Hartman, Tom Doyle, Jerry Stark, Sam Jost, William Peirpont, Victor Welsh, William Hichinson, Harry Arthur, Bud Stark, Jim Smith, Ed Glenz, Charles Copeland, Al Swanke, Fred Courtwright, and in uniform, Police Inspector Carroll Tichenor. (Oregon Historical Society, CN021606)

6

A PRECINCT GROCERY

For a year or so, contributions including food and clothing were delivered to the Central Police Station, until it was overflowing the lobby . . . so it was decided to move the Sunshine Division to the East Side precinct and place it under Lt. Tichenor. In this station, there was a second floor not being used for anything except perhaps the meetings of the Police Reserves.[1]

—Ray Carr, 1975

Both the Central Precinct and the East Second and Belmont location (formerly Joe's Cash Store) needed to be free of the unpredictability and clutter of the Sunshine Fund activities. So the 1926 move to the second floor of Portland Police East Precinct on Seventh and Alder was a relief to everyone. Most importantly, Inspector Tichenor could administer the program from his own office. The lobby and the day-to-day activities of Central Precinct could proceed without the complicating hospitality involved in accommodating generous givers, or needy recipients, or piles of food, clothing, and supplies.

Concurrently, the term "Vigilante" began to take on a new and somewhat negative meaning in Portland and society in general as a word that represented someone willing to take matters into his own hands at any cost rather than a person vigilant to the immediate needs of the city. Therefore, at the request of Inspector Tichenor, on March 17, 1926, the Portland City Council, voted to change the name of the

Grocery Store of the Sunshine Division
Headquarters on Seventh and Alder, c. 1927.
(Oregon Historical Society, #CN007806)

Portland Police Vigilance Reserves to the Portland Police Reserves.[2]

At the new Seventh and Alder location, the now Portland Police Reserves could more easily include the duties of the Sunshine Fund in their volunteer routine. To make the site more accommodating for merchandise and distribution, City Commissioner John Mann personally donated labor and materials for the building of shelves and the counters for storage and processing. The improvement made more available space for the seven to ten volunteers as well as the reserves, who were buzzing about, sifting and sorting through inventory.[3]

The floor space of the new headquarters was 60 by 110 feet, with a small office in one corner of the room. Primarily, the space was devoted to the storage of food, clothing, and furniture. According to the *Northwest Police Journal,* "the same order and system exists as would be found in any organized business firm—the well-arranged stock on the shelves reminded one of a merchandise store more than anything else."[4]

The city, with the enthusiastic support of Mayor Baker, provided, without charge, the square footage necessary to run the operation, as well as the salary of Inspector Tichenor and one seasonal assistant. Tichenor, in turn, used the opportunity to increase the program to a year-round emergency relief organization with an advisory board, an annual financial report, and community volunteers in addition to the reserves and officers.

Within the initial administrative function, the Board of Directors for the Portland Police Reserves and the Board of Directors for the Sunshine Fund were one and the same. No positions were honorary or incidental, although the list was a "Who's Who" of the established civic community. The first administrative elements consisted of Mayor George L. Baker, Chief of Police Leon. V. Jenkins, Inspector C. H. Tichenor, and Tichenor's best friend, E. E. Ratelle, as secretary. The first six reserve sergeants consisted of Maynard Cole, Paul J. Closset, Victor Welsh, E. L. English, C. Eitelman, and Norman A. Thompson. The First Advisory Board of the Portland Police Reserve consisted of R. J. Belland, George E. Frost Jr., Barnett H. Goldstein, Harry DeWitt, J. W. Jones, John H. Luihn, L. R. Robinson, A. R. Sawtell, C. J. Van Blaricom, and Frank E. Weed.

In the midst of the new sense of permanence after the move to Seventh and Alder, Inspector Tichenor publicly declared the need for emergency food relief to be a perennial one with the following remarks in the *Sunday Oregonian,* May 9, 1926:

The real thought behind the police relief bureau is to broadcast a little of the Christmas spirit throughout the year.

There is hunger and want in the city in May as there is in December. This truth has been brought vividly to us in our Christmas work. We have learned that the spirit of giving and the desire to make others happy during the holiday season has resulted in a feast for the needy at that time, though that famine has continued for the rest of the year.

Through the generosity of the public and the merchants at Christmastime, largely because the need for help has been given such wide publicity through the broadcasting of the Hoot Owls, we have received more than enough food to fill our Christmas baskets. Notwithstanding that last year the police and reservists and Hoot Owls distributed two heavily laden baskets to hundreds of needy families on Christmas day, instead of just one basket as in previous years, we had a supply of food left over. This served as a nucleus for our reserve. It has been added to by further donations.[5]

—Inspector C. H. Tichenor, 1926

In 1926, the procedure for the year-round distribution of food to a given family was triggered by one of two things. The first, a police officer on patrol noticed that a family was in need of assistance and would take action. The other, a call would come in to East Precinct from a community member suggesting that an officer check into a family's circumstances. The daily bulletin distributed to police officers from the office of the chief of police had permanent instructions in the margin. Officers were told that "Any officer knowing of any needy family in their respective districts, kindly get the initial and name of the head of the family, the ages and the sex of the children and submit report of same to Inspector Tichenor at Sunshine Headquarters. . . ."[6]

In either case, uniformed officers would go to the home and inspect to determine, as best they could, if "want" truly existed. The officer would return to Seventh and Alder, report the situation, gather the necessary food boxes and household items from the volunteer staff, then deliver them to the home in his patrol wagon. If the officer did not have time to tend to the situation or make the delivery, Inspector Tichenor would call one of the Vigilance Reserves living near the neighborhood of the family to conduct the delivery.

Clothing Store of the Sunshine Division
Headquarters on Seventh and Alder, c. 1927.
(Oregon Historical Society, #CN104204)

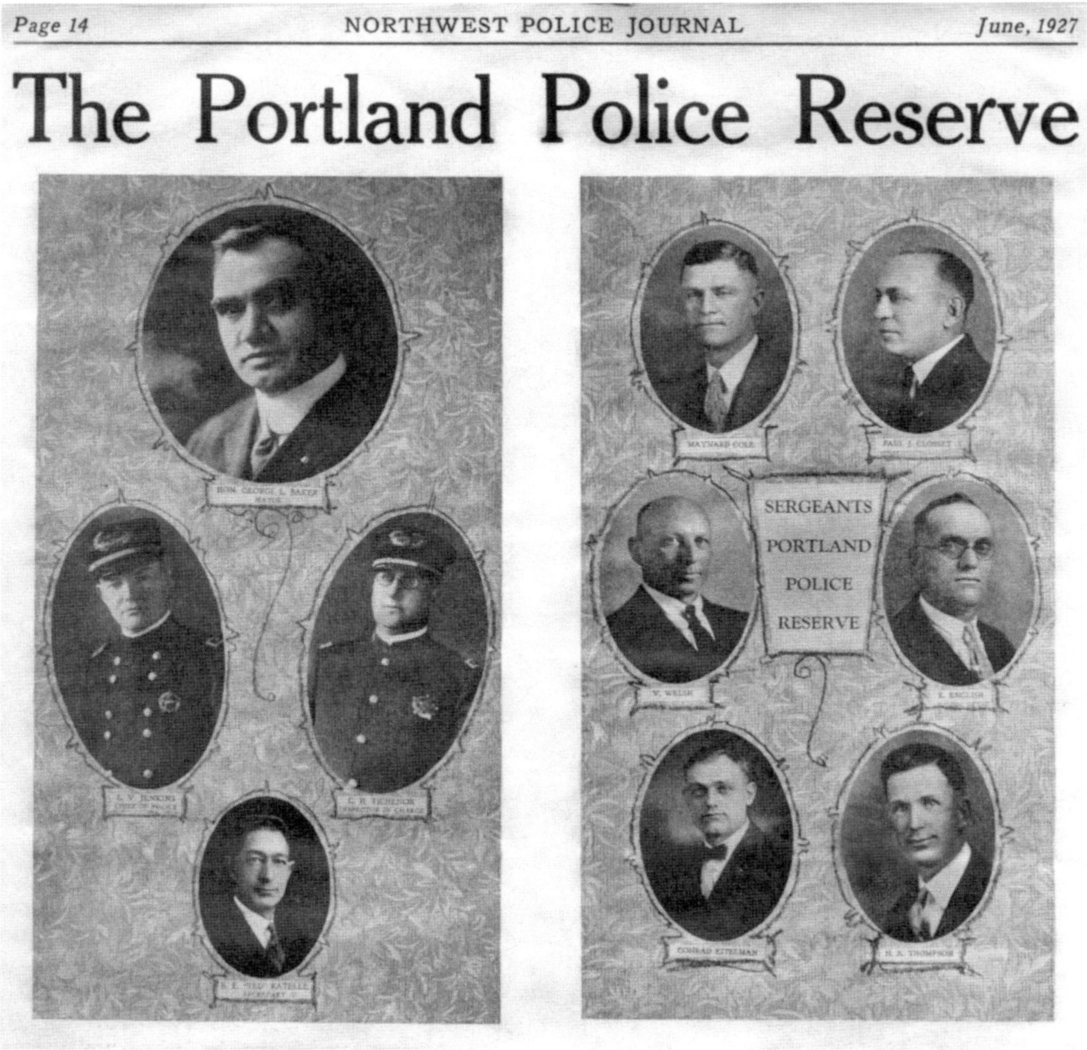

Page 14 NORTHWEST POLICE JOURNAL June, 1927

The Portland Police Reserve

HON. GEORGE L. BAKER
MAYOR

L. V. JENKINS
CHIEF OF POLICE

C. H. TICHENOR
INSPECTOR IN CHARGE

E. E. "TED" RATELLE
SECRETARY

SERGEANTS
PORTLAND
POLICE
RESERVE

MAYNARD COLE

PAUL J. CLOSSET

V. WELSH

E. ENGLISH

CONRAD ETTELMAN

N. A. THOMPSON

The Police Department administrators of the Vigilance Reserves included Mayor George L. Baker, Chief Leon V. Jenkins, Inspector C. H. Tichenor, and E. E. (Ted) Ratelle as secretary. The volunteer community members assigned to be the six sergeants consisted of Maynard Cole, Paul Closset, Vic Welsh, E. English, Conrad Ettelman, and Norm A. Thompson. (City of Portland, SPARC, SSD Scrapbook Collection, A2000-026)

The Advisory Board consisted of high-profile businessmen in the community including John "Jack" H. Luihn, Frank E. Weed, Harry DeWitt, C. J. Van Blaricom, L. R. Robinson, R. J. Belland, Barnett H. Goldstein, A. R. Sawtell, George E. Frost Jr., and J. W. Jones. (City of Portland, SPARC, SSD Scrapbook Collection, A2000-026)

Much to the dismay of many social workers through the years, officers were more or less bold in their inspection of the homes of the possible recipients. Some would enter the home and speak to the family; some would walk around the kitchen opening cupboards and asking questions as if he were conducting a benevolent criminal investigation where food relief was the consequence.

More often, the common description of the "inspection" by the officer—generally told from the perspective of a child who is now a great deal older, was that of a patrol wagon pulling up to the front of the house or apartment. The uniformed officer would get out of a large black car and walk up the sidewalk slowly, to indicate by casual demeanor that there was no police emergency. It also gave him a chance to look over the yard and exterior for indications of fuel needs. He would then knock upon the door, which was generally opened very cautiously (if at all) because the resident often had no idea what was happening. The officer would then explain that the Police Bureau was informed that the family might be in need of some relief assistance and would ask to come in.

At first, the children were apprehensive but later felt at ease with the officer as he opened cupboards while asking questions about fuel and clothing in a friendly manner. Generally, by the end of the visit, the officer would announce that he would return in a few hours with the necessary provisions to get the family by for a few days or weeks.[7] Not long after, he would return with the foods and household items needed to help the family.

After a few days, when the issues of hunger had subsided, the family was revisited and asked about their employment needs. The police officers, in the words of Inspector Tichenor, would get the "low down" on the situation. If there were able-bodied men or women in the family, the police would find work for them, largely through the reservists, who included businessmen and employers in many lines. If the need was the result of some circumstance that called for continual help and relief, the case was turned over to the Public Welfare Bureau.[8]

Ed Wilson, later the representative of the Meat Cutters Union to the community and the Sunshine Fund shared his reflections of the early years:

> *My first experience with the Sunshine Division was about 1924. I think I was 23 or 24. There was a family, I used to drive a butcher wagon, and I delivered meat on 24th and Thurman, 24th and Vaughn. I used to deliver meat there to a family that lived on the corner house there. Next door was a family that was destitute. They had nothing. She had a couple of kids. They had nothing. They never had fuel to heat the house and there was snow on the ground. This woman told me about this lady next door and says, "Gosh, Why don't you call the Sunshine Division." So, I reported her to the Sunshine . . . to the police, and they came out there and brought her some food and brought her some wood. They had Model T Fords in them days you know, and top hats, hard hats. They fixed them up. The cops themselves went out and bought the kids a pair of slippers. A lot of people don't know that, the way the Sunshine Division come up.*[9]
>
> —Interview, Ed Wilson, 1987

Although Inspector Tichenor was the only uniformed officer working for year-round pay on the Sunshine Fund, from December 5 to December 25, 1926, Chief Jenkins assigned uniformed patrolmen H. Rekdahl and W. B. Stram to the task of gathering donations from local merchants. They were given one of the Black Maria paddy wagons for pick-ups and spent the days working their way down a long list of donation sites.

Patrolmen H. Rekdahl (left in uniform) and W. B. Stram (right in uniform) pose for the *Oregonian* newspaper as grocerymen and volunteers load donated items into the paddy wagon, Black Maria, 1927. (Oregon Historical Society #CN021611)

Portland Police Reserve Dance, Bellands Hall, November 8, 1926. E. E. Ratelle (second from left, front row), Chief L. V. Jenkins (fifth from left, front row), George L. Baker (center), Fire Chief Holder (fourth from right), Commissioner C. A. Bigelow (third from right), Inspector C. H. Tichenor (second from right). (City of Portland, SPARC, SSD Collection, A2000-026)

According to the second official annual report of the Sunshine Fund of the Police Department, Hoot Owls, and Police Reserves (donated by the accounting and auditing firm of Sawtell, Withington & Company), the food relief program provided a one-week supply of food to 1,050 families over the period of February 25, 1926, to May 13, 1927. In the previous annual report, the time span of accountability was shorter due to the newly established bookkeeping records of Inspector Tichenor, showing a total of 370 families from October 31, 1925, to February 25, 1926. Even with the shorter duration of the earlier report, the numbers show a dramatic increase in services for the holidays if one compares the downtown location to East Precinct.[10]

As publicity for the Sunshine Division mounted, so did public awareness and therefore demand. In 1926, the three local papers began to fill with stories of the destitution that hit the poor of Portland in two-year cycles before the official dawn of the Great Depression. The police were first to draw attention to the harsh realities.

Occasionally, numerous reports of need would flood into the Sunshine Division following a newspaper article that featured assistance given through their services. With clustered requests coming into the office, the newspapers would again exhort the business community to respond generously to the need for donations, thus creating a self-perpetuating cycle of empathy-generated provisions. Fortunately, the merchants helped to create a steady balance between supply and demand, offering those who were in need of emergency relief an opportunity for temporary assistance.

Newspaper accounts delighted in the testimony of the beat officers who interviewed with a colorful and somewhat cynical outlook, offering a certain flare to the account of the plight of the needy. In general, the police apparently enjoyed more social freedom to comment on family situations compared to the more tactfully reserved employees of faith-based charitable enterprises that were extensions of religious organizations. One officer, after investigating the family situation of a father who abandoned a wife and five boys (the oldest a paraplegic), proclaimed to the newspaper reporter, “Husbands who leave their wives ought to be subjected to the whole Spanish Inquisition,”[11] thus offering a quote not generally characteristic of the Salvation Army or of representatives of St. Vincent De Paul. Donations poured in to the Sunshine Division the next day, designated specifically for that family in the name of the officer who articulated his frustrations toward wayward fathers.

The first permanent location of the Division within a precinct and within the administrative flowchart of the Police Bureau encouraged the establishment of many policies that grew into long-standing traditions of the Sunshine Division and the Police Reserves.

• The title "Sunshine Division" appears for the first time in an annual report from Seventh and Alder, with the word "Sunshine" coming from the phrase coined by Bishop Sumner of the Hoot Owls within the "Rainbow Division" of his part in the show.

• "Division" emerges for the first time from the fluent use of the word in city government—earmarking a level of status within city government.

• The name "Portland Police Reserves" is established permanently under Inspector Tichenor.

• Official police-sponsored food distribution became an established year-round activity rather than seasonal.

• And most of all, an official procedure for the inspection of homes and the distribution of food by officers and reserves is established with the reserves offering support in times of high demand.

In a speech broadcast over KGW radio during the Hoot Owls' 1926 Christmas Eve show, E. E. Ratelle, secretary for the Portland Police Reserve, summarized the progress of the Police Bureau's commitment to the hungry for that year.

> *Due to the fact that Inspector Tichenor is so heavily engaged at the Sunshine Headquarters supervising the filling of baskets for the needy ones of our city, I am at his request going to tell you briefly some of the main points of interest pertaining to the Sunshine Charity work, conducted by the Hoot Owls and the Portland Police Department in conjunction with the Police Reserves.*
>
> *Approximately 500 families will be served. They represent over two thousand men and women and children. Each family will receive two large market baskets carefully filled, to meet the requirement of each case. Each allotment of food will exceed $10.00 in actual value.*
>
> *To give you an idea of the magnitude of this work, there will be on hand at seven o'clock tomorrow morning, 20 meat cutters, between 200 and 300 automobiles and about 350 people*

W. B. Stram posing for the *Oregonian* with
Vigilance Reserves loading baskets into Reserve automobiles.
(Oregon Historical Society #CN021608)

Inspector Carroll Tichenor, his son Earl Tichenor,
Carla Bush (niece of E. E. Ratelle), and
E. E. "Ted" Ratelle with several Chinook salmon
caught at the mouth of the Sixes River near Cape Blanco.
(City of Portland, SPARC, SSD Collection, A2002-009)

to assist in delivering the allotment of food to each needy family.

These have been carefully checked by the police, under able supervision of Inspector Tichenor and cleared through the confidential exchange, thereby overcoming practically all possibility of duplication.

Due to the heavy Hoot Owl program I am only able to give you these few facts, but in conclusion and on behalf of Inspector Tichenor and the Police Reserves we wish to express our deep appreciation for the fine contributions of money, food-stuffs, clothing, etc. Also, our grateful appreciation for the helpful and efficient cooperation accorded us by Mayor Baker, the Hoot Owls of the Oregonian, *Chief Jenkins, the entire Police Department, and all those who have contributed in any way.*

Without the cooperation just mentioned, which has been given so freely and effectively, Insp. Tichenor and his entire force of Police Reserves, could not have possibly coped with the heavy but worthy demands upon them.[12]

—E. E. Ratelle, Secretary,
Portland Police Reserves, 1926

Later in his speech Ed Ratelle went on to describe the contents of the deliveries. The first basket was filled with a respectable quantity of food consisting of flour, canned milk, soup, pineapple, fruit, and beans, with packaged cereal, crackers, macaroni, two pounds of sugar, two pounds of beans, two pounds of prunes, two pounds of rice, two pounds of mixed nuts, two pounds of candy, and one pound of coffee. In the second basket there were three loaves of bread, one cake, a bag of apples, one dozen doughnuts, one pound of butter, twenty pounds of potatoes, one bag of candy, one package of meat, one bag of cookies, and an assortment of toys. Also, families were given fuel and clothing if the need was dire.[13]

Ed Ratelle was the first secretary of the Police Reserves. An avid sportsman, he and Inspector Tichenor would often set out to hunt for game to be placed in the Sunshine food baskets. The year 1926 brought forth 420 pounds of salmon at the mouth of the River Sixes by the skilled trolling hands of Inspector Tichenor, his son Earl Tichenor, Ratelle's niece Miss Carla Bush, and Mr. Ratelle. The following year,

Nearly 400 ducks and geese were obtained for the Sunshine Division, the relief organization of the Portland Police, the KGW Hoot Owls, and

the Police Reserves, by a dozen Portland nimrods, who returned yesterday from a five-day trip to the game bird lakes and rivers near Klamath Falls, Oregon.

Immediately on their return, the hunters turned over their bag, which numbered some 350 ducks in addition to a score or more of Geese, to Lt. C.H. Tichenor in charge of Sunshine Division headquarters on Seventh and Alder.

The nimrods also turned over to Lt. Tichenor an owl, shot by eleven-year-old Jim Barnes, the son of Marion Barnes, resident game warden at Klamath Falls, Oregon, who acted as a guide for the Portlanders. The Owl was given to the Hoot Owls by the youngster, and Lt. Tichenor will make the presentation Friday night. . . . Those making the trip included Captain Lewis, Patrolmen Evans, Bobell, Roberta, and Sergeant Huntington of the Police Bureau: Maynard Cole and Elmer Sapher of the Police Reserves and A. J. Haas and others. [14]

The casual nature in which the article offers the information that the owl will be presented Friday night, implies the relationship between the Hoot Owls and the local community, as well as eleven-year-old Royal Order of the Hoot Owl membership card recipients from as far away as Klamath Falls. Listeners within hundreds of miles understood that the Hoot Owls were on the radio Friday night as certainly as any other favorite radio program. And sure enough, the dead owl was presented to the Hoot Owls on the air with the affected tongue-in-cheek reverence so often employed, as if the animal were a trophy awarded within a secret fraternal game club.

The following November a bear was brought to Inspector Tichenor after it had been shot by police reservist-apple farmer Maynard Cole. Cole said that there are some who will not exactly mourn the death of "Mrs. Bruin," among them being George Baccrich and Otto Castrow of the Gillen-Cole Company. Cole described, "The two hunting pheasants in the Cole orchard a week ago last Sunday, and also hunting apples, ran across the bear all-of-a-sudden like, and were said to be still running." [15] The proceeds from the sale of the bear were given to the Sunshine Division for the purchase of food and household items.

~

Portland Police Vigilance Reserves at the Merrykhana Parade, June 17, 1927. (City of Portland, SPARC, SSD Scrapbook Collection, A2000-026)

Portland
DEALER
227-A

▷ and ▽ Portland Police Vigilance Reserves at the Merrykhana Parade, June 17, 1927. (City of Portland, SPARC, SSD Scrapbook Collection, A2000-026)

Although caution dictated between the sworn police officers and the reserves in the earliest years of the establishment of the Vigilantes, by 1926, a fraternal tie began to develop between the two entities, particularly with regard to the poor. Often on banners and in conversation, the Police, the Reserves, and the Hoot Owls were called the "Sunshine Trio."

In a gesture of solidarity toward sworn police, the Portland Police Reserves, numbering 107, agreed to sign a petition to put a fire-police wage increase on the ballot for the May 1926 election, and pledged $1 each toward the campaign fund to put the request before the public. Within two weeks, petition signatures were sufficient to place the proposed increase on the ballot, which passed.

Merrykhana

Giving humor the chance to address the complexities of a civilian police interacting with a sworn police organization, the Portland Police Reserves entered themselves in the "Applesauce Division" of the Portland Rose Festival second annual Merrykhana Parade, June 17, 1927. To chants of "Applesauce, Applesauce" roaring from the crowd seated within the Multnomah Stadium, several dozen Portland Police Reservists staggered into the arena with oversized hats and stars, human-sized fishing nets, donkeys adorned in blue wool uniforms, and paddy wagons filled with dignitaries, KGW Hoot Owls, and policemen. The Reserves were granted first place in their division, and the parade enjoyed greater attendance than the Grand Floral Parade.

Loading a truck of food donated by Fred Meyer
at his SW Fifth and Yamhill location, December 15, 1932.
(Oregon Historical Society #CN104111)

7

EMERGENCY ASSISTANCE REDEFINED

As documented in the annual report of the fourteen-month "fiscal year" of March 31, 1928, to May 31, 1929, the Sunshine Fund of the Portland Police Department, Hoot Owls, and Police Reserves, services were at their highest and increasing daily. Although the impact of the worldwide economic depression of the 1930s had yet to become a nationwide reality, Portland seemed ahead of schedule; the number of calls for service at the Sunshine Division was ominous.

> *During the fourteen months under review approximately 4,272 persons were served with food* [approximately 1,068 families],[1] *212 deliveries of fuel, and approximately 195 persons furnished with articles of wearing apparel.*
>
> *Approximately 800 families were served with food on Christmas Day* [3,200 persons] *and the cost of supplies furnished during the period at wholesale amounted to approximately $5,800.00.*
>
> *The average weekly appeals for relief during the winter months were in excess of 20 families. . . .*[2]
>
> —Annual Report of the Sunshine Fund of the Portland Police Department, "Hoot Owls," and Police Reserves, March 31, 1928–May 31, 1929

In the fiscal year ending March 31, 1930, the year of the October 1929 stock market crash, the stunned

Cartoon of the "Biggest Barrel in the World," 1933.
(City of Portland, SPARC, SSD Scrapbook Collection, A2002-009)

businessmen of the Portland Police Reserves managed to pull together enough emergency food for 633 families (2,532 people). They also gathered and dispersed 199 deliveries of fuel; 222 persons were furnished with winter clothing; and more than 830 unemployed families were served with holiday food baskets on Christmas Day.

As the economy plunged, the work of the Sunshine Division became more serious and more intense. In the following annual report for the ten-month time period of May 31, 1930, to March 31, 1931, the numbers skyrocketed again.

> *In spite of the extraordinary demands that were made upon the resources of the Division, Lt. Tichenor and his aids were able to add to the Savings Account, bringing the amount so invested up to $10,000.00 with accumulated earned interest of $110.75. . . . Some idea of the magnitude of the Division's operations may be gained from the following statistics . . . 1,727 families were served food* [approximately 6,900 people] *750 Christmas baskets were distributed; 760 families were furnished fuel; and clothing was given to 1,151 families* [approximately 4600 people]. *Wheelchairs were furnished to 18 cripples. Contributions of fuel amounted to approximately 8 tons of coal and 75 cords of wood.*[3]
>
> —Annual Report of the Sunshine Fund of the Portland Police Department, "Hoot Owls," and Police Reserves, May 31, 1930–May 31, 1931

With Portland unemployment statistics often at 30 percent, what was once a benevolent representation of the kindness of police officers and businessmen became a civic entity pulled into a cyclone of local economic turmoil. In a city of 301,815 citizens, by 1932 more than 60,000 workers were without an income.[4] Persons capable and willing to provide for themselves were starving and exposed to the elements, and they were not alone. What's more, they had only scratched the surface of what was to come.

Variations in Theme

Due to the arrest of what were ordinarily law-abiding citizens who, for reasons of economic discouragement, had turned to crime or alcohol, another new phenomenon began to occur at Seventh and Alder. Men officially called "trusties" were allowed to fulfill their time of community service by assisting with the sorting and packaging of Sunshine Division inventory. Generally, Inspector Tichenor would call the local municipal judge and inform him that Sunshine needed some workers. One could easily tell when the judge had received that call, for soon the Black Maria paddy wagon would be shuttling those sentenced for lesser crimes, such as shoplifting and "vagrancy," down to Seventh and Alder to assist the inspector.

The tradition carried on for years, until decades later, under Commander Bud Lewis,[5] trusties would intentionally have themselves "arrested" and removed from the street during the holiday season because they so enjoyed the companionship of working together with the reserves to serve the poor—not to mention a hot meal, a new set of clothes, and no sermon. Every year, the trusties would catch up on the happenings of others, see who was missing and wonder where their comrades might be.

Occasionally, according to Commander Lewis, the police squad cars would intentionally locate one specific sidewalk resident of the downtown area who was quite massive in stature. He was valued because he was soft-spoken, kind, and had the capacity to lift an entire side of beef and hang it on a ceiling hook. At Christmastime, whenever the trusty would see familiar officers coming his way in the patrol car, he would wave, stand up, and climb into the back seat. One year, the trusty was sorely missed when he could not be located, only to learn that he had passed away from alcoholism. A brief moment of silence was offered at the Reserves' weekly meeting to commemorate the loss of a friend, fellow worker for the hungry, and a man of unique strength.

Although not obligated, this writing will preserve the privacy of the trusties. With that in mind, it is interesting to observe that trusties were proud to pose for newspapers and media events during their "incarcerations." Evidence of such can be located in Portland newspaper archival collections from the 1930s, 40s, and 50s.

Court-ordered trusties were not the only ones who participated in the distribution of food during the Depression of the 1930s; hundreds of nonincarcerated citizens offered their services when they could not find work, hoping to give meaning to their occupational skills. The following is a 2002 donor letter to the Sunshine Division concerning the relationship between her father and the Sunshine Division of the late 1920s and into the 30s:

> . . . *My father whose skills were in the grocery business, simply could not find work. His morale*

THEY FURNISH THE BRAINS

In a 1935 promotional booklet written and supported by the Friends of the Sunshine Division, the Board of Directors is profiled as a no-nonsense group of businessmen who offer their organizational expertise to the efforts of Captain Tichenor.

Photos (left column): Mayor Joseph K. Carson; Portland Police Chief H. M. Niles; board member Paul R. Kelty, editor of the *Morning Oregonian;* Thomas E. Shea, editor of the *News Telegram;* and Donald J. Sterling, managing editor of the *Oregon Journal.*
Photos (right column): board member J. "Jack" Luihn, manager of Sealy-Dresser Co.; Inspector L. V. Jenkins; Captain C. H. Tichenor; board member C. W. Jerome, editor of the *Portland Bulletin;* board chairman Fred Spoeri, division commercial representative, Pacific Telephone; and R. A. Hudson, president of Hudson and Duncan & Co., one of Portland's leading wholesale grocers.
(City of Portland, SPARC, SSD Collection, A2000-026)

was low . . . my mother suggested to my father that he go to the Sunshine Division and offer his services in stocking and dispensing donated groceries in exchange for a weekly streetcar pass. . . . His offer was welcomed, and he immediately took over the job of warehousing incoming and outgoing donated grocery items. . . . After a while, he was given $5.00 a week in addition to a [$1.25] *streetcar pass. At least he had somewhere to go and something to do. . . . our family managed to save enough of that money to cover the down payment on a small "Mom and Pop" grocery store . . . the store thrived under my father's management . . . it* [the Sunshine Division] *enabled my father to regain his self respect and finish out his life owning a very successful grocery store of his own.*[6]

In addition to food, clothing was an essential element of the services offered in the 1930s. Many people lived in makeshift homes constructed of cardboard, newspapers, and scrap wood. Layers of clothing meant survival throughout the winter months. One couple registered on a 3-by-5-inch record of services with the Sunshine Division had the address of their single-family residence crossed out and then replaced with the words "Sullivan's Gulch," telling the sadly common story that they had once lived in a house. As well, the only donations registered on the card were for a single male, which makes tragic sense, as Sullivan's Gulch was generally a homeless community for men. For reasons unknown, the family no longer shared the same home.

Sullivan's Gulch, a shantytown located just east of where Interstate 84 now approaches Interstate 5 in Portland eventually became the inspiring element for the creation of the Housing Authority of Portland due to ". . . the shortage of safe and sanitary dwellings in said city available to persons of low income. . . ."[7] But for the 30s, a common Sunshine Division donation history for a man in "The Gulch" involved a pan for sponge baths, a coat, pants, underclothes, blankets, and briquettes.[8]

To supplement the need for warm blankets, Mrs. Tichenor organized quilting bees in an effort to produce warm, layered bedding for persons without heat. Active in the work were Mrs. C. O. Gates, Mrs. Basil P. Bert, Mrs. D. D. Story, Mrs. E. L. Patton, Mrs. Anna M. Wagnon, Mrs. E. J. Pieco, Mrs. E. R. Harris, and Mrs. Ida Knudson.[9] Later Mrs. Tichenor's efforts were reflected and continued by a group of Reserve, Police, and SSD Board wives and community members called the Sew and Sews. The Sew and Sews

Roger Woodyard of Woodyard Brothers Inc. stands in his
2825 Northeast Woodstock store with one of the early food
barrels placed by the Sunshine Division of the 1920s.
(City of Portland, SPARC, SSD Collection, A2002-009)

An unidentified man, Chief Harry Niles, and Captain H. Circle admire the can display in the downtown precinct during what came to be known as Can Day. Harry Circle, a grocer before becoming a police officer, arranged the display to be a cityscape of Portland. (City of Portland, SPARC, SSD Collection, A2002-009)

gathered often to make layettes, repair quality clothing, and to enjoy each other's company.

In 1932, the Sunshine Division surpassed any and all expectations for emergency relief, with 3,751 families receiving food throughout the year and 850 families receiving Christmas dinners. The Division was a major barrier between many families and complete despair, with the resources and cooperation of the Hoot Owls, the Reserves, and the Police Bureau at full tilt. Its efficiency and capacity to turn around donations at the speed at which they came in was unprecedented, and remains so if one considers the per-capita statistics of Portland at the time.

Services extended far beyond food, clothing, and bedding to involve a stove-rehabilitation project that turned around 240 refurbished stoves, 305 fumigated mattresses, 253 quilts, 98 sets of dishes, 54 wheelchairs, 59 baby carriages, and thousands of shoes—not to mention mush and fire fuel for Tusko the elephant.

Tusko

Tusko, the "Biggest White Elephant in Captivity," was in trouble. His master was in jail for drunk driving. It was a snowy winter night, and his barn at the foot of Main on the east side of the Willamette was cold. The police had only one choice—a choice often made by Portland officers when dealing with a citizen at risk—call the Sunshine Division to feed Tusko and stoke his furnace. Even Portland elephants of the 1930s could count on the police when hardship prevailed.

When bail brokers Ed Mosier and William Brenner went to the barn to inspect the living security that Tusko's not-so-sentimental owner offered as collateral for bail (Tusko himself) they found two Sunshine Division Police Reserves playing cards by a roaring fire while Tusko munched on warm mush.[10]

Beyond the Owls

The year 1933 was the last year the KGW Hoot Owls would regularly promote the Sunshine Division Christmas Campaign. Their individual careers began to flourish and expand, leaving many of the talented businessmen unable to commit to the time involved for such a popular radio show. Two years before, in 1931, the Hoot Owls program had officially gone off the air, with only occasional guest appearances for special occasions including promotions for the Sunshine Division. In 1933, their regular seasonal activities ended as well. The concern for what might happen to the Sunshine Division without the Owls created an influx of creative gestures of support by local artists such as the organist and songwriter of RKO fame, Jean Anthony.

Appearing on the title page of the sheet music for Jean Anthony's "Sunshine Song" are Tillie and Jackie Rollo in the company of Police Chief Jenkins. Jenkins was the first chief to guide and promote Captain H. Circle in his benevolent activities with uniformed police officers in the 1920s. Mr. Anthony wrote the song in the east before bringing his radio artist skills to Portland. Inspired upon hearing of the activities of the Sunshine Division, he quickly rewrote the words of his song, printed 10,000 copies, and donated 45 percent of his proceeds to the Division.

Remember many are hungry,
many are blue,
Waiting for you to help the sunshine through
Give for Sunshine with a happy smile . . .
You know the Sunshine Division,
in sunshine or rain,
Friend of the friendless of Portland fame . . .[11]

In a flyer inserted within the sheet music, Captain Tichenor thanked the purchasers of the song with a brief note:

Friends of the Sunshine Division, We hope that every home in the city will cherish this "Sunshine Song." ever reminding you of the sunshine that you, our friends are spreading through our Division. . . .

—Captain C. H. Tichenor

Even with the best efforts and intentions of local individuals, without the Hoot Owls, it became necessary for the Sunshine Division committees to take a more active role in sustaining public awareness. Fortunately, KGW was owned by the *Oregonian* newspaper, which offered columns upon columns of coverage of the activities of the Sunshine Division before and after the Hoot Owls. Most importantly, the Advisory Board of the Sunshine Division at the time that the Hoot Owls disbanded was a collection of highly regarded and powerful men in the Portland business community.

The Board included Chairman Jack Luihn, manager of Sealy-Dresser Co.; Fred Spoeri, division commercial representative of Pacific Telephone & Telegraph Company; Paul Kelty, editor of the *Morning Oregonian;* Donald Sterling, managing editor of the *Oregon Journal;* Tom E. Shea, editor of the *News Telegram;* C. W. Jerome, editor of the *Portland Bulletin,*

Cover sheet for Jean Anthony's "The Sunshine Song." (City of Portland, SPARC, SSD Collection, A2000-026)

and R. A. Hudson, president of Hudson Duncan & Co., one of Portland's leading grocers. Such broad-based community representation involving persons in a position to publicize the Division manifested a steady stream of creative promotional ideas. Those ideas inspired consistent donations from both the working class and local business owners.

The Big Barrel Committee

On December 11, 1933, the Sunshine Division "Big Barrel," built voluntarily by the P. T. Ainge Company under the supervision of the "Big Tree Committee" of the Sunshine Division, was unveiled as the new monument of the downtown location for food collection for the Christmas season. Economic hardships rendered impractical "The Biggest Christmas Tree in the World" and "The Sunshine Fairy Land" of the previous two years, because the earlier attractions required thousands of incandescent lights. The Big Barrel was equipped with lower voltage but modern amenities such an anonymous, masked member of the Advisory Committee adorned in a red slicker trimmed in white fur who preferred, for the time being, to be addressed as "Santa." Furthermore, the Electrical Products Company donated neon lights and an electric eye, a new curiosity of modern science, set to trigger flashing lights and a bell-bar whenever a person entered or exited the barrel.

The Big Barrel stood over 16 feet, 6 inches, tall and was 12 feet wide at the girth. It symbolically represented more than two hundred barrels distributed in grocery stores and markets throughout Portland, as well as the tradition of doing so since the mid-twenties. The master of ceremonies for the event was a locally admired Ray Carr, a gifted advertiser who effectively sustained many of the promotional elements of the Sunshine Division when the Hoot Owls disbanded. After Carr's introduction, Paul R. Kelty, editor of the *Oregonian,* shared his thoughts, "Rain augers well for such an enterprise as this one, because I can't recall a single dedication of the 'Big Tree' during which there wasn't rain, and every single year brought success to the organization."[12]

Big Barrel Committee member Ray Carr stands at the microphone in front of the "Biggest Barrel in the World" in 1933, while the curious wander by the downtown receiving depot. The barrel stood 16 feet, 6 inches tall, was 12 feet in diameter at the "waist," and weighed 5 tons. (Oregon Historical Society #CN63434)

△ Pack Night as it is and as it has been for eighty years. Boxes rest in four layers. (City of Portland, SPARC, SSD Collection, A2000-026)

▷ Pre-Christmas delivery, post–Pack Night warehouse. A trusty from the jailhouse, smoking a cigarette, walks between four layers of boxes and several dozen donated sides of beef. Soon, the representatives of the Meat Cutter's Union will arrive to complete the final cuts of meat for delivery the next day, December 25. (City of Portland, SPARC, SSD Collection, A2000-026)

8

THAT SHALL HE ALSO REAP

The Sunshine Division demonstrated consistent and continual progress supported by both yearly and year-round campaigns to gather food, financial contributions, and household necessities in the eight years following 1933. With the headquarters above the East Precinct on Seventh and Alder overflowing with goods, rent for another location simply called the Neustadter Building was reported in the 1936 annual report as an additional warehouse for inventory.[1] Addressing the need, the Police Bureau moved the Sunshine Division into the abandoned Albina Police Precinct on 38 Northeast Russell Avenue. (Originally, the building housed the Albina City Hall until it was annexed by the City of Portland.) Although the new location was a marked improvement, space was still limited, and the SSD Board of Directors began to advocate ways to build a warehouse on an adjacent lot. The hope was to ensure a more effective distribution process for household items and to create space during seasons of high inventory.

With a growing awareness of the permanent nature of the Sunshine Division, funding for a warehouse was approved and appropriated as one of the 125,000 public buildings completed nationally under the Emergency Relief Appropriations Act. Groundbreaking ceremonies took place May 5, 1938, as Paul Kelty of the Sunshine Advisory Board, cigar in hand, watched Oregon State WPA Director E. J. Griffith turn the first shovel. Within forty-seven days, a two-story, 75-by-95-foot warehouse of brick, tile, and concrete

The Sunshine Division board members make their municipal presence known in a photo shoot within the City Council Chambers under Mayor Joseph K. Carson, 1941. Front row from left: Dean Knowles, C. M. Pomeroy, unknown, John Bredemier, Ira Cobe, Carroll Tichenor, unknown, Jack Luihn, Leon Jenkins, Geo. Pearson, unknown, Norm A. Thompson. Back row from left: Kenneth Cooper, William A. Bowes, Earl Riley, Joseph K. Carson, Fred L. Peterson, Jacob Everett Bennett. (City of Portland, SPARC, SSD Collection, A2002-009)

construction was completed in the vacant lot directly adjacent to the new Russell Avenue Headquarters.

Construction of the $14,000 structure carried out by the Works Progress Administration cost $8,407 for labor and $473 for sand and gravel. The Pacific Coast International Association of Law Enforcement Officials sponsored $3,000, with the balance covered by the city of Portland.[2]

Upon completion, Mayor Joseph K. Carson arrived to lay the final cornerstone at 2:00 P.M., on July 20, 1938.[3] Representing the WPA was E. E. Withrow, assistant director of WPA operations in Oregon. Assistant Director Withrow turned the building over to Mayor Carson, who, in turn, gave the keys to Chief of Police Harry M. Niles,[4] who then gave the keys to Captain Tichenor. Mayor Carson "wielded the trowel" and installed a marble marker; copies of Portland daily newspapers, a dedicatory message and resolutions by the City Commissioners were deposited behind the marker.[5] The time capsule has since been recovered, its contents now located at the Stanley Parr Archive and Record Center in Portland. The contents of the capsule also included a photograph of J. H. Luihn, SSD Board chairman also serving as the State Relief chairman; Paul Kelty, member of the Sunshine Advisory Board; and an impishly grinning Captain Tichenor who supervised shovel-in-hand WPA Administrator E. J. Griffith.

After reading the following proclamation, Mayor Carson placed the document behind the cornerstone as the WPA band closed the ceremony with "Happy Days are Here Again," the antithetical theme song for the Roosevelt administration's victorious 1932 campaign for the presidency.

> *ON THIS DAY IS BEING LAID THE CORNERSTONE OF THE NEW WAREHOUSE AND HOME OF THE SUNSHINE DIVISION, CHARITY ORGANIZATION OF THE PORTLAND POLICE DEPARTMENT AND THE PORTLAND POLICE RESERVES. WE THE UNDERSIGNED, THE MAYOR AND THE COMMISSIONERS OF THE CITY OF PORTLAND, UNDER WHOSE ADMINISTRATION THIS STRUCTURE HAS BEEN PLANNED AND ERECTED, TAKE THIS OCCASION TO CONSECRATE IT TO ITS NOBLE PURPOSES OF CHARITY.*
>
> *THEREFORE, BE IT RESOLVED, that no finer hope can be expressed than that the SUNSHINE DIVISION, under this new roof, carry on with ever increasing enthusiasm and efficiency the work of mercy which has brought it national and international fame—a work which has shown*

Portland to be a city where the unfortunate are not forgotten—a work which has turned many a desperate father and son away from thoughts of crime, which has clothed thousands of children for school and play and work, which has provided fires for thousands of homes that otherwise would have been without heat, which has fed the hungry, clothed the ragged, sheltered the homeless;

THEREFORE BE IT FURTHER RESOLVED, that it is the wish of the undersigned that this work shall continue under this new roof so long as the need shall remain.[6]

The proclamation was signed by Portland Mayor Joseph K. Carson, Portland Commissioner of Finance R. E. Riley, Commissioner of Public Works Ormond R. Bean, Commissioner of Public Affairs Jacob E. Bennett, and Commissioner of Public Utilities Ralph Clyde.

The new warehouse was a long-awaited advantage for the Division, as insufficient space was a constant issue. At last, there was one location for what has become one of the most long-standing and significant traditions of the Sunshine Division—a phenomenon simply called Pack Night.

For the entire history of the Division, compiling the Christmas food baskets was the pinnacle of the year's activity with close to three hundred volunteers. When space was limited, the preparation of boxes or baskets had to be done in stages and at varying locations. In the weeks before every Christmas, donors and contributors would converge on the Division dropping off tons and tons of food whenever and wherever it was manageable. With one very large warehouse, the coordination was greatly simplified. Even then, on Christmas Eve 1938, the new Russell Avenue Warehouse had little or no walking space by the time more than 2,600 food boxes in four layers, wall to wall, were ready for delivery Christmas Day.

A focus upon the productivity of the Sunshine Division is incomplete unless one takes into account the poverty it represents. Unfortunately, when more people were served, it often meant that more persons were overwhelmed with uncertainty and had to live moment to moment.

More significantly, increased productivity within the Sunshine Division was a manifestation of a coinciding focus of city government, the business community, and local advertising interests. Although persons in need of emergency assistance were certainly a part of the economic dynamics of the early 1940s, Roosevelt's

Groundbreaking ceremonies for the new Sunshine Division Warehouse involved, from left, J. H. "Jack" Luihn, State Relief Chairman; Paul R. Kelty, Sunshine Advisory Board; Captain C. H. Tichenor; and WPA Administrator E. J. Griffith with the shovel. (City of Portland, SPARC, SSD Time Capsule, A2002-009)

WPA-sponsored Sunshine Division
Warehouse under construction, 1938.
(City of Portland, SPARC,
SSD Scrapbook Collection, A2002-009)

WPA laborers proudly pointing
out their efficiency, 1938.
(City of Portland, SPARC,
SSD Scrapbook Collection, A2002-009)

Mayor Carson placing the time
capsule in the new WPA-built
Sunshine Division Warehouse, 1938.
(City of Portland, SPARC,
SSD Scrapbook Collection, A2002-009)

The interior of the new WPA-built
Sunshine Division Warehouse, 1938.
(City of Portland, SPARC, SSD Scrapbook Collection, A2002-009)

declaration of war on December 8, 1941, was an external magnet of social conscience and energy.

Although Roosevelt's First and Second New Deals were vital to those fortunate enough to participate in the thousands of projects within the Northwest, unemployment never fell below 14 percent in the region until the beginning of World War II. In fact, the migration of displaced farmers and workers from other portions of the country greatly complicated the unemployment statistics of Portland, especially when WPA projects were completed and workers were left unemployed and on the doorstep of the Sunshine Division once again.

With the mayor and the City Council unwilling to recognize the desperate need for low-income housing, throughout the late 30s more than six thousand persons lived in shelters deemed "uninhabitable" by the U.S. Department of Commerce.[7]

Steadily, the Sunshine Division, along with other relief organizations, continued to provide the household amenities and foodstuffs specific to the needs of those living in extreme poverty and cold, while the Portland Planning and Housing Association continued to pressure city government for adequate living conditions to meet the needs of the underemployed.[8]

Not until the Kaiser Corporation reluctantly threw together the Vanport and Guilds Lake housing projects in 1941, knowing that federal funding for war-effort housing would become available in 1942, did Portland become the last major city on the West Coast to approve a Housing Authority.[9] Until late 1942, it was common for a shipyard or war-related industrial worker to come to town and be unable to find adequate housing, making employed homelessness common in Portland for the early war years. It was none too soon that the city and the industrial centers would begin to create housing developments, as Portland had already become infiltrated with migrant manufacturers working to complete the lend-lease war materiel contracts won by Henry Kaiser.

Once local war-related manufacturers and the city began to effectively address housing issues, two dynamics in the early 1940s brought changes to the services of the Sunshine Division. First, the need for emergency provisions to the poor began to decrease due to lower unemployment rates—even in single-parent households. Second, by 1943, nearly 50 percent of the Portland Police Bureau officers were engaged in military service, while the older businessmen of the Police Reserves were generally involved in organized community war efforts. Although emergency food assistance was most likely in demand, the Police Bureau was stretched beyond its limits to provide basic police services to the community, leaving no resources for non-law-enforcement duties and services.[10]

In addition, Captain Tichenor's health prevented him from participating in the 1941 Christmas campaign with the same energy he usually offered. By March he found it difficult to work at all. Friday, May 1, 1942, Captain Carroll Holt Tichenor died unexpectedly at Hahnemann Hospital of complications from prostate surgery. The city of Portland, the Police Bureau, the local business community, and the citizenry were stunned. His life symbolized Portland's unusual approach to the usual. Rarely did a day go by that at least one of the major papers did not have a story or two concerning the dichotomous character and intrigue of Portland's policeman who fed the poor. The overwhelming feeling was that the heart of the city had been cored. With the entrance of the United States into another world war as the final punctuation of an economically debilitating decade, Tichenor's death was an extreme discouragement.

Honorary pallbearers at Captain Tichenor's services conducted at the A. J. Rose Funeral Home were a veritable Who's Who of the legendary Portland "establishment," the Police Bureau, and the local philanthropic social services community. The list included Mayor Earl Riley and City Commissioners W. A. Bowes, Ralph C. Clyde, Fred L. Peterson, and Kenneth Cooper. Also included were Paul R. Kelty, Tom E. Shea, J. H. Luihn, Ira Cobe, Philip H. Parish, Barnett Goldstein, Donald J. Sterling, Reverend H. F. Gelvin, C. W. Jerome, R. A. Hudson, S. M. Vranson, Emil Gelinsky, Chief of Police Harry M. Niles, Inspector Jenkins, C. A. Inskeep, H. A. Lewis, W. C. Epps, Frank Ervin, J. J. Keegan, John H. Schum, James Fleming, Patrolman E. R. Biggs, and Captain H. A. Circle.

The active pallbearers were Tichenor's Police Reserve Lieutenants H. D. Jensen, Norman A. Thompson, Dean H. Knowles, C. M. Pomeroy, J. F. Hill, and George Pearson.

For days hundreds of letters to the editor were sent to all the major newspapers in the area describing the meaning of Captain Tichenor and his life's work. Businesses inserted commemorations dedicated to Captain Tichenor in the corners of their advertisements.

The man to replace Captain Tichenor, who was wise enough to know that there was no replacement for Captain Tichenor, was Captain Walter A. Tyler.[11] In a quiet ceremony with Chief Niles on May 27, 1942, Captain Tyler received his appointment. A few days later, he commemorated Captain Tichenor in a letter to the *Oregon Journal,* and gently articulated the changes to come.

> *When I was appointed the head of the Sunshine Division, the other day, Chief Niles said, "I want to bring the Division close to the police department." . . . Although I will give full time to the Sunshine Division, it is my duty to attend all the meetings of the Captains and share in the discussions. . . . Improvement in employment has decreased calls as compared with last year. But in a city the size of Portland, there are always emergencies that may be due to death or the unfitness of the breadwinner, loss of jobs, sickness, injuries. Sometimes we have to help the families of newcomers who came here for work but have nothing to live on until pay checks begin . . . this is what the citizen ought to do who is panhandled on the street by the moocher who begs the price of food for a cup of coffee:*
>
> *Refer him to the Sunshine Division, Second and Oak. For those who deserve it, there will be two meals and a bed for the night.* [12]

As can be discerned by the referral to "Second and Oak" Captain Tyler was to be assigned and stationed to Central Precinct, while the volunteer staff and the paid staff of the Sunshine Division were to continue their work in a pared-down organization on Russell. The number of families served in 1941 was not particularly different than in 1940, especially considering the fact that Tichenor was not feeling well. The decrease in Christmas boxes only went from 1,479 in 1940 to 1,353 in 1941, and the decrease in annual food allotments went from 1,219 in 1940 to 1,005 in 1941.

The real challenge in furnishing the Sunshine Division with a captain was due to the exodus of officers and ranking personnel from the Bureau into the military. According to Portland Police historian Ralph O'Hara, more than 50 percent of the officers and reserves on the street were drafted or enlisted in the service. As much as the Bureau wanted to leave a captain at the Russell Avenue Warehouse, the complete replacement of Tichenor was impossible. As well, the "roll-up-you-sleeves and get to work" conviction that swept the community placed little patience with those who "mooched," in the words of the new Commander Tyler. "Two meals and a bed for the night should suffice," was the no-nonsense

Editorial obituary for C. H. Tichenor from the *Oregonian,* May 4, 1942.
(City of Portland, SPARC, SSD Collection, A2002-009)

Christmas 1945 with Inspector L. V. Jenkins and Captain
Walter A. Tyler holding baskets before delivery.
(City of Portland, SPARC, SSD Collection, A2000-.026.1)

Captain Walter A. Tyler, appointed commander of the Sunshine Division after the death of Carroll H. Tichenor in 1942. (City of Portland, SPARC, SSD Collection, A2002-009)

wartime motto of the Division when Captain Tichenor was out of the picture.

In December 1942, the Annual Christmas Drive of the Sunshine Division was cancelled. In the words of Jack Luihn, "Our load is lighter because of better conditions in the city, and we don't want to take any of the Big Barrel Committee members from their defense activities." He went on to say that the Division would accept and disperse voluntary contributions. The Christmas basket deliveries for the year totaled 233 families even without the campaign.[13] Deliveries were made in Sunshine trucks and in private cars operated by volunteers.

As the war progressed, the number of persons served by the Sunshine Division decreased almost to nothing. By 1944, only eighty-five families received Christmas baskets, and thirty-one families received food allotments apart from the holiday season, but the Division remained. Although it served very few people, it was never completely eliminated. Even though services were nearly nonexistent due to the number of policemen overseas and reservists who were consumed with the war effort, Portland could not imagine itself without a Sunshine Division.

In 1945, Inspector Jenkins and Captain Tyler happily carried food baskets for a picture in the newspaper, surrounded by enough food for 178 families. The effort was certainly meaningful to those who needed the support, but the quantity distributed was the second-smallest total quantity since 1922. The positive irony remained; low numbers for the Sunshine Division meant a better economy and more favorable numbers regarding unemployment.

In Portland, the "Liberty and Victory Ship Capital of the Country," any person who wanted to work and had the ability to work, could find work. Portland-area shipyards constructed the world's largest war housing cities, including nurseries, hospitals, post offices, play areas, schools, shopping centers, administrative buildings, and cafeterias. Permanently or temporarily single heads-of-household could work and support an entire family with extraordinary assistance and convenience. After a full shift, a worker could pick up the family meal from the cafeteria, then pick up the children from the on-site school and day-care facilities. High production was essential and Kaiser strove to provide the simplicity workers needed to meet the demands. The once-discouraged and underemployed workers of the Portland area—male and female—were making headlines around the world with their phenomenal capacity to lay

Captain Walter A. Tyler, appointed commander
of the Sunshine Division after the death
of Carroll H. Tichenor in 1942.
(City of Portland, SPARC, SSD Collection, A2000-026.20)

In 1945, an elated group of Sunshine Division Board members and friends celebrating the first Sunshine Division postwar get-together as community-oriented energies could return to local concerns. Front row: C. M. Pomeroy, Dean Knowles, George Pearson, Captain W. A. Tyler, Harry Gelvin, Chief Harry Niles, Barnett Goldstein, Inspector Leon Jenkins, Jack Luihn. Back row: Ira Cobe, Emil Gelinsky, Fred Hill, Al Mauser, Steve Vranson, Norman Thompson. (City of Portland, SPARC, SSD Collection, A2000-009)

the keel of a Liberty Ship and have it ready to sail ten days later.[14]

Persons who turned to the Sunshine Division during the war were those who were not already permanently assisted by a social service agency or those who could not work temporarily. When they were interviewed for assistance, the questions were always presented in this way, "Have you tried to locate work? If so, when do you get paid? And, if not, why not?"

After the war, things at the Sunshine Division began to pick up again, but Tyler was still assigned to Central Precinct, supervising the Sunshine Division effort over the phone and with frequents visits for photo shoots and administrative duties. As calls for service began to increase, it became less feasible to delegate the duties to volunteers and reserves. It appeared that with the new mayor, Dorothy McCullough Lee, in office, changes were to come.

The staff of the Portland Police Sunshine Division in 1947:
Mae Tardiff, Stuart Sloan, William Smith, Captain W. A. Tyler,
William Wiley, William Kennedy, and Mae Koehn.
(City of Portland, SPARC, SSD Collection, A2000-009)

9

FULL CIRCLE

It is a relatively unknown fact that Captain Circle initiated the Sunshine Division. Captain Tichenor accomplished the task of running the Division so effectively during his two decades of service that the actual story of the beginning was lost and the legend of Tichenor as founder was propagated. Captain Circle didn't concern himself with straightening the record. Apparently, he was glad that the work continued, and content in the knowledge that he was instrumental.

The actual beginning of the Sunshine Division is of great importance because it rests upon the reality that it was established by police officers. The infrastructure of giving was later preserved and sustained by the city, the reserves and the advertising community, but the box of donated change rested first on Captain Circle's desk, and street cops, frustrated by the cruelty of poverty, filled that box. The remaining story is eloquent and essential, but not first.

Circle's decades of relative silence over his role in the establishment of the Sunshine Division are no indication of his willingness to set matters straight when a situation made it necessary. As captain of Central Precinct, the public and his officers could rely on his sense of fairness and concern for their welfare.

When Portland Police historian Ralph O'Hara left to serve in the South Pacific during World War II, Captain Circle, working downtown at the time, promised that Ralph could return to his rookie position at Central Precinct when the war was over. Upon his

Captain H. A. Circle
(Courtesy of the Portland Police Museum)

return, Ralph headed straight downtown and walked up to Harry's desk in the middle of the precinct. (The well-liked Captain Circle preferred not to have a private office, while most persons of his rank and responsibility were behind closed doors.) After a joyous and vigorous handshake, Captain Circle promised to take care of the paperwork. Moments later, Officer O'Hara witnessed something rare; he witnessed an extremely angry Captain Circle.

The word from the chief's office was that Officer O'Hara would be assigned to night shift in the north end of town, one of the most dangerous areas to work at the time. Because Ralph was a late-returning veteran, the positions at Central were already filled; there were no openings. O'Hara soon found himself trailing behind a fuming Captain Circle to the chief's office, concerned that he would never work for the Bureau again if things did not go well. Waiting outside, he could hear Captain Circle offer Chief Niles a loud, uncensored discourse on why Officer O'Hara would be assigned to day-shift at Central. Chief Niles proceeded to assign O'Hara to day-shift at Central.[1]

As Captain Circle drew near the end of his exceptionally long career in law enforcement, Mayor Dorothy McCullough Lee, aware that Captain Circle had initiated the Sunshine Division, assigned him from Central Precinct to commander of the Sunshine Division in 1949—twenty-five years after it had been given to Inspector Tichenor. Her regular attendance at the Sunshine Division Board of Directors meetings, and her words spoken within those meetings, indicate that she believed the Division to be a vital force in her hope to improve her city, and to improve the residents' wavering trust in the police force. In the minutes of her third Sunshine Division board meeting in six months, Mayor Lee expressed her thoughts without notes.

> *Mayor Lee stated that the fine public relations created by the officer on the beat being able to give immediate help to those in distress gave them the respect and good will of the people.*[2]

From September 1, 1949, to his retirement on July 1, 1952, Captain Circle was the official commander of the Sunshine Division.[3] Under Captain Tyler, postwar calls for assistance had quadrupled, going from a total of 441 families in 1946 to 1,811 in 1949. Mayor Lee decided to devote a full-time staff person to the Sunshine Division effort.[4] Captain Tyler had successfully reactivated the Division since the war and was quite involved, considering his many responsibilities, but it was considered best to have a commander on site at Russell Avenue. Circle was near retirement, willing to "return," and had a long-term interest in the effort. He was an obvious candidate as the new mayor's administration settled in.

Upon his retirement after forty-nine years of service to the Portland Police Bureau, when asked what he believed to be the most important accomplishment of his long, well-decorated career, Captain Circle would say, "the founding of the Portland Police Sunshine Division in 1921."[5]

The Present

At present the Portland Police Sunshine Division serves more than fifteen thousand persons per holiday season with food for their Christmas dinners. Two Pack Nights keep 175 volunteers busy in a high-spirited assembly line. For the days following, six hundred volunteers, reserves, police officers, and businessmen deliver more than four thousand holiday food baskets. To avoid duplication, in 2001, the Sunshine Division established the Holiday Assistance Network Data System (HANDS) online data base making it possible for every organization in Multnomah County that provides holiday food boxes to register the names and addresses of the people they are helping.

In addition to the holiday boxes, the Sunshine Division furnishes emergency food relief to twelve to fifteen thousand people per year. In 2002, 1.2 million pounds of food went through the warehouse now located at 687 North Thompson.[6] If emergency food is needed after hours, boxes are located in all of the five Portland police precincts to be delivered or picked up if necessary.

In addition to serving clients directly, each year the Division offers tens of thousands of pounds of food at no cost to the Salvation Army, St. Vincent de Paul, Snow Cap, FISH Emergency Services, William Temple House, and an additional forty organizations. To replenish food supplies, as of 2003, every major and independent grocery chain in the Portland metro area delivers food to the warehouse throughout the year.

For clothing needs, the Division provides full sets of clothing to nearly two hundred children per year through the Issy's Kids program. If a police officer believes children need clothing when their clothes are taken in as evidence or if they have none, the officer can get a voucher and go shopping with the child for underwear, shoes, outer clothing, and a coat.[7]

The combination of the business community, the Portland Police Bureau, and local broadcast companies continues to weave together a joint effort to provide for those with an emergency need for food.

For eighty years, the collaboration has made possible an unusual circumstance. If a person living within the city of Portland is suddenly unable to buy food—call the police.

(City of Portland, SPARC, SSD Scrapbook Collection, A2000-026)

NOTES

Chapter 1 — The Poor Man Beside Me

[1] Ralph Waldo Emerson, *Nature Addresses: Man the Reformer.* (Cambridge: Riverside Press, 1876), 227.

[2] Edward Reid, "Police to Retire, Ending Half-Century Era," *Oregon Journal,* 13 April 1952.

[3] "Police Cheer Needy Family," *Oregon Journal,* 11 December 1921, 1.

[4] "Police Cheer Needy Family," *Oregon Journal,* 11 December 1921, 1.

[5] Annual Report of the Sunshine Fund of the Police Department, "Hoot Owls," and Police Reserve, 1925. City of Portland, SPARC, SSD Collection, A2000-026.

[6] Charles Tracy, "The History of Portland's Sunshine Division," 1979. City of Portland, SPARC, SSD Collection, A2000-026. Dr. Charles Tracy of Portland State University penned a brief history of the Portland Police Sunshine Division with the support and assistance of Sergeant Ralph O'Hara of the Portland Police Department in 1979. The history was as complete as could be expected considering the lack of primary documentation available at the time. Several interviews were conducted and the remaining research for the project has laid much of the groundwork for the timetable of this work. The documentation for the entire project is located at the Stanley Parr Archives and Record Center for the City of Portland in its own series.

[7] "Police Congratulated for Relief Activity," *Oregon Journal,* 24 December 1921, 1.

[8] Frederic Jaher, *The Urban Establishment.* (Urbana: University of Illinois Press, 1982), 8–11.

Chapter 2 — The Portland Police Vigilantes

[1] Carl Abbot, *Portland: Planning, Politics and Growth in a Twentieth Century City.* (Lincoln: University of Nebraska Press, 1983), 73.

[2] E. Kimbark MacColl, *The Growth of a City: Power and Politics of Portland, Oregon 1915–1950.* (Portland: The Georgian Press), 140.

[3] Abbott, 73.

[4] Carl Abbot, one of Portland's foremost historical scholars writes in *Portland: Planning, Politics and Growth in a Twentieth Century City,* that George Luis Baker was a genuine self-made man who started shining shoes and selling newspapers in San Francisco at the age of nine. He came to Portland in 1889 and over the next twenty years built a successful career as a downtown theater owner and impresario. He represented a downtown ward on the City Council between 1898 and 1900 and again from 1907 to 1913, building a political organization held together by his own personality. He started the first of four consecutive terms as mayor in 1917.

[5] Phillip Silver, *George Luis Baker: An Inquiry Into the Methods and Psychology of Municipal Leadership.* 1926. Multnomah County Library, Special Collections, 352.0791 B173S. Phillip Silver was a courageous Doctoral candidate at Reed College, willing to take

on the mayor of Portland for his extremism and administrative methods.

[6] MacColl, 157–158.

[7] MacColl, 139–140.

[8] "Mayor Baker to be Police Chief," *Portland Telegram,* 5 January 1921, sec. 1, p. 18.

[9] In an important decision made by the Interstate Commerce Commission in Washington, D.C., determined that railroad companies could not charge the same rate of service for the water-level rail lines into Portland as mountain lines into the cities of Puget Sound. Implementation of this decision began July 1, 1921 and resulted in increased shipping of agricultural and inland products from the Northwest.

[10] "Mayor's Message and Annual Reports, Portland, Oregon," 1921. City of Portland, SPARC, SSD Collection, A2000-002.

[11] "1922 Tax Commission Report," Oregon State Archives, Salem, Oregon. At the time, taxation and funding decisions for law enforcement were made at the state level. The Oregon State Tax Commission was mandated to oversee tax equalization laws implemented in 1906. Apparently, they found the budget for the Portland Police Department to be inequitable as compared to what citizens around the state had to pay for law enforcement, deeming the City of Portland responsible for its additional per-capita costs.

[12] "New Police Patrol Systems Discussed," *Oregon Telegraph,* 15 November 1921, p. 9.

[13] "Mayor Wrathy at Police Plan of Tax Board," *Oregon Telegraph,* 22 December 1921, Eve. Ed., Section 1, p. 1.

[14] "Mayor Wrathy at Police Plan of Tax Board," *Oregon Telegraph,* 22 December 1921, Eve. Ed., Section 1, p. 1.

[15] "Feeding and Clothing the City's Unfortunates," *Northwest Police Journal,* January 1931.

[16] Unidentified newspaper article, circa 1919. City of Portland, SPARC, SSD Scrapbook Collection, Scrapbook 1919–1931, A2000-026. The scrapbook series of the Portland Police Sunshine Division at the Portland City Archives consists of 16, 12" x 20" scrapbooks compiled by the paid or volunteer staff of the Division and occasionally by the wife of SSD Commander Tichenor. They are complete and chronological, and occasionally have the date of the article and the newspaper clipped off. I use this one as the only one within this manuscript without a date. It appears to be from the *Oregonian.*

[17] "Detective and Martin Clash," Police Reserves Scrapbook, 1917–1931, City of Portland, SPARC, SSD Collection, 2001.

[18] City of Portland, SPARC, Portland City Council Charter, 10-07-21/2, 1903.

[19] "Vigilantes Organize to Combat Sedition," *Oregonian,* 26 January 1918, p.13.

[20] "Governor Lauds American Idea of Civilian Reserve," *Oregonian,* 2 November 1919, p. 8, c. 3.

[21] Christopher Capozzola, "The Only Badge You Need is Your Patriotic Fervor: Vigilance, Coercion and the Law in WWI America," *The Journal of American History,* 88.4 (2002): 76 pars, 28 June 2002. http://www.historycooperative.org/journals/jah/88.4/capozzola.html.

[22] Portland City Ordinance #40608, January 1922. City of Portland, SPARC.

[23] Memo, Scrapbooks 1919–1931. City of Portland, SPARC, SSD Collection, A2002-009. In addition to newspaper articles, the PPB SSD scrapbooks contain memos, orders, receipts, photographs, invitations, announcements, and a variety of items pertaining to important chronological events.

[24] Portland Police Vigilance Reserves and Portland Police Reserves Records. Norman A. Thompson, 10-07-21 /2 8023-01, City of Portland, SPARC.

[25] Portland Vigilance Reserve Applications, City of Portland, SPARC, SSD Collection, 2001, A2000-026.

Chapter 3 — A More Human and Heartborn Task

[1] Although the term "Black Maria" could be misconstrued as racially offensive, its name is not of a racially based origin. This sardonically affectionate nickname for vehicles in the Portland Police Paddy wagon fleet is tied to their resemblance to a hearse, and their vocation of carrying people away. The upside: criminals were being taken to jail, rather than the typical destinations of coffins.

[2] "Police Carry Cheer to Poor Families," *Oregonian*, 24 December 1922: 1.

[3] Carl Abbott, *Portland: Planning Politics and Growth in a Twentieth Century City.* (Lincoln: University of Nebraska Press, 1983), p. 73.

[4] C. H. Williams, "Cheer is Carried Into Every Home," *Oregonian,* 12 December 1922.

[5] "Christmas Joys Already Tasked," *Oregonian,* 22 December 1923.

[6] "Two Families in Need, Men Seek Work of Any Kind, Aid Asked for 17 Grown People and Children by Members of Police Bureau," *Oregonian,* 23 January 1923.

[7] "Charity Spreads Christmas Day," *Oregonian,* 25 December 1923, p. 1.

[8] E. Kimbark MacColl, *The Growth of a City: Power and Politics in Portland Oregon 1915–1950.* (Portland: The Georgian Press, 1979), 140.

[9] "Big-Hearted Police Spread Real Cheer." *Oregonian,* 24 December 1923: 1. The reporter of this article also added that Captain Circle had been delivering food baskets for seven years. This is the only resource thus far that implies a uniformed police food delivery starting date of 1916.

[10] E. Kimbark MacColl writes in the previously cited *Growth of a City: Power and Politics of Portland, Oregon,* that Dorothy McCullough Lee was a reluctant reformer (648-649). For nearly two years before her bid for the mayoral position, her peers and acquaintances hounded her to run for the office based upon her independent spirit and her determination to do what she thought to be "right" rather than politically expedient. According to MacColl, Dorothy McCullough Lee possessed a distinguished background in both family antecedents and professional experiences. Her maternal grandfather, Thomas Hill, was a prominent painter of western scenes whose "Driving the Last Spike" now hangs in the California State Capitol Building in Sacramento. Her father, Dr. Frank McCullough, was the fleet surgeon of the U.S. Navy before World War I. When she settled in Portland in 1924 as a bride of 23 with a recent law

degree from University of California, the native San Franciscan was Oregon's youngest woman lawyer. Her husband, an industrial engineer with the Standard Oil Company of California, had been assigned to the Portland office.

Chapter 4 — Owls, Goats, Dignitaries, and Such Matter

[1] "Broadcasting from KGW," *Oregonian,* 30 January, 1923.

[2] Radio Service Bulletin, #57 3 January 1922, Para. 57, p. 55.

[3] "Hoot Owls Stage Birthday Festivity" *Oregonian*, 27 December 1924 p. 6. c. 1.

[4] Dean Collins, *Hoot Owl Classics*, Volume One. The Rainbow Division. (Portland: The Mercantile Press, 1928). City of Portland, SPARC, SSD Collection.

[5] Mrs. Norm Thompson Jr. Interview with Lori Shea Kuechler, 2 August, 2002.

[6] Harry Grannatt. *Hoot Owl Classics*, Volume Two, The Rainbow Division. (Portland: The Mercantile Press, 1932). City of Portland, SPARC, SSD Collection, A2000-026.

[7] Norm Thompson Jr. Interview with Lori Shea Kuechler, 2 August 2002.

[8] Blanc, Mel. "That's Not All, Folks." (Warner Books: New York 1988), 17.

[9] Blanc, 18.

Chapter 5 — The Sunshine Fund

[1] Ray Carr was and is still considered to be one of the establishing elements of the advertising and promotional practices of the Sunshine Division. His leadership as a working member of various committees of the Division coupled with a myriad of advertising and promotional ideas earnestly facilitated by Jack Luihn promptly replaced the Hoot Owls without a detectable decrease in revenue.

[2] Ray Carr to Isabel Hoyt, 1975. City of Portland, SPARC, SSD Collection, A2000-026.

[3] *Oregon Journal,* Home and Family, Sec. 2, 16 December 1971.

[4] "Police, Hoot Owls Carry Good Cheer," *Oregonian,* 26 December 1924.

[5] Michael L. Kurtz, *The Challenging of America 1920–1945,* (Arlington Heights: The Forum Press, 1986), 42–43.

[6] "Big Banner Helps in Sunshine Drive," *Oregonian,* 7 December 1925.

[7] C. H. Tichenor, "Ledger Book," circa 1927, City of Portland, SSD Collection, A2000-026.

[8] *The Portland Sunshine Division*, Promotional Booklet, (Portland, 1935). City of Portland, SPARC, SSD Collection, A2002-009.

[9] Gerry Frank. Interview with Lori Shea Kuechler, 29 October 2002.

Chapter 6 — A Precinct Grocery

[1] Ray Carr to Isabel Hoyt, Memos and Correspondence, City of Portland, SPARC, SSD Collection, A2000-026.

[2] Portland City Council Meeting Vol. 71, p. 534, Ordinance #49071. City of Portland, SPARC.

[3] "Police Supply Depot Aids Many Needy With Food Left Over After Christmas," *Oregonian,* 9 May 1926.

[4] "Feeding and Clothing a City's Unfortunates," *Northwest Police Journal,* February 1931, 38.

[5] "Police Supply Depot Aids Many Needy With Food Left Over After Christmas," *Oregonian,* 9 May 1926.

[6] City of Portland, SPARC, SSD Scrapbook Collection, A2000-026, Bulletin 337, 1st Bulletin, 2:00 P.M., 3 December 1926, Portland Police Department, John T. Moore Acting Chief, 1926.

[7] City of Portland, SPARC, SSD Collection, Recipient Correspondence File, A2000-026.

[8] "Police Supply Depot Aids Many Needy With Food Left Over After Christmas," *Oregonian,* 9 May 1926.

[9] Ed Wilson. Interview with Charles Tracy and Ralph O'Hara, 1987. Tracy/O'Hara Research Series, City of Portland, SPARC, SSD Collection, A2000-026.

[10] Annual Report, The Sunshine Fund of Police Department, "Hoot Owls" and Police Reserves. City of Portland, SPARC, SSD Collection, A2000-026.

[11] "Cries of Destitute Poor Fill Ears of City Police," *Morning Oregonian,* 13 December 1926.

[12] Police Reserves Scrapbook #1, Ed Ratelle Speech, 24 December 1926, City of Portland, SPARC, SSD Collection, A2002-009.

[13] Police Reserves Scrapbook #1, Ed Ratelle Speech, 24 December 1926, City of Portland, SPARC, SSD Collection, A2002-009.

[14] "Portland Nimrods Bag Early . . .," *Oregonian,* 20 March 1927.

[15] "Police will Sell Bear," *Oregonian,* 15 November 1927.

Chapter 7 — Emergency Assistance Redefined

[1] Occasionally, bracketed numbers will reflect one of two things. When a number of families served is given, the following bracketed numbers will offer an estimated number of people served based upon a four-member family size. If a number of people are given, then occasionally a bracketed figure of families or households is given in addition. Each year and season, the number of baskets for each household was different depending upon the resources, community collective need and the time of year. Generally, family size was four and two baskets per family routine procedure unless the situation was extenuating.

[2] "The Sunshine Fund of Police Department, 'Hoot Owls' and Police Reserves" Annual Report, FY 31 March 1928–31 May 1929. City of Portland, SPARC, SSD Collection, A2000-026.

[3] "The Sunshine Fund of Police Department, 'Hoot Owls' Police Reserves, May 5, 1931. Annual Reports," City of Portland, SPARC, SSD Collection, A2000-026.

[4] Mildred Schwab. *Portland Fact Book 1981,* Bureau of Planning, City of Portland, Oregon. City of Portland, SPARC.

[5] Leland S. "Bud" Lewis, Interview with Lori Shea Kuechler, 2001. It is important to know that the trusties helping within the Sunshine Division truly found the Division to be a safe environment in which to serve the community at a time when helping others was often difficult to accomplish for personal or legal reasons. In addition, documentation of the "unofficial" relationships between the Sunshine Division and many in the street community

is impossible to locate. According to Commander Lewis, no one participated against their will, and the assistance was very helpful. Commander Bud Lewis was born to farmers in Alberta, Canada. His father and mother, Victor E. and Marie M. Lewis, decided to live farther south and moved to Portland, Oregon, where he began his thirty-year career with the U.S. Postal Service. Bud Lewis went to Benson Tech and then joined the Oregon National Guard's 41st Division, at the age of sixteen, for what was supposed to be one year. After serving in action in the World War II New Guinea theatre including Biak, he was reclassified to the Military Police at the Portland Army Base. Following his discharge, Lewis became a patrolman for the Portland Police Bureau, worked a variety of positions and was later promoted and assigned to the Sunshine Division, serving as commander from June 13, 1963, to September 12, 1973.

[6] Donor letter to Sunshine Division Commander Sergeant Wayne R. Kuechler, 1998–present, Name to be kept in confidence.

[7] Resolution #22081, Adopted by City Council, December 11, 1941. City of Portland, SPARC.

[8] 3" x 5" Donation Record Cards, circa 1925–1955. In process, City of Portland, SPARC, SSD Collection.

[9] "Comforters for the Poor," *The News Telegram,* (Portland, Oregon), 21 November, 1930.

[10] "Tusko Goes Bond To Rescue Master From Prison Cell," *News Telegram,* (Portland, Oregon), 2 February 1932. "Tusko Provides Bail to Free Owner from Jail," *Oregon Journal,* 2 February 1932.

[11] "The Sunshine Song" 1932, City of Portland, SPARC, SSD Collection, A2002-026.

[12] "Big Barrel Lights Flash Goodwill," *Oregonian,* 15 December 1933.

Chapter 8 — That Shall He Also Reap

[1] "Annual Report, The Sunshine Division of the City of Portland, 1936," City of Portland, SPARC, SSD Collection, A2000-026.

[2] "Annual Report, The Sunshine Division of the City of Portland, 1938," City of Portland, SPARC, SSD Collection, A2000-026.

[3] The mayors for the early years of the Sunshine Division were: George L. Baker, 1917 to 1933; Joseph K. Carson Jr., 1933 to 1941; Earl Riley, 1941 to 1949; Dorothy McCullough Lee, 1949 to 1953.

[4] The position of Chief of Police was held by the following in the early years of the Sunshine Division. Leon V. Jenkins, 1919–1938; Burton K. Lawson, 1933–1934; Harry M. Niles, 1934–1946; Leon V. Jenkins (again), 1946–1947; James Fleming, 1948–1949; Charles P. Pray, 1949–1951.

[5] "New Sunshine Building Officially Taken Over," *Oregon Journal,* 22 July, 1938.

[6] WPA, Russell Avenue Dedication, City of Portland, SPARC, SSD Collection, A2002-009.

[7] Ralph E. Clyde, Memorandum to the Council, 17 June 1938, Jesse Short File, Box 2. (Portland: Oregon Historical Society).

[8] Carl Abbott, Portland: *Planning, Politics and Growth in a Twentieth Century City.* (Lincoln and London: University of Nebraska Press, 1983) 117. Early in 1938, a joint committee of the Planning Commission and the Housing Code Commission recommended in favor of a Portland

Housing Authority by a split vote of 7 to 4. After stormy hearings in which conservative councilmen heckled the housing reform advocates, ignored their statistics and proclaimed that public housing was "unadulterated Communism entirely," the council submitted the question to an advisory referendum. The only effective support came from the Planning and Housing Association. The referendum lost in defeat at the polls after a city-wide campaign that played upon the fears that lower rent and property values would be a direct result of its passage.

[9] E. Kimbark MacColl, *The Growth of a City: Power and Politics in Portland, Oregon.* (Portland: The Georgian Press Company), 575.

[10] Ralph O'Hara, Interview with Lori Shea Kuechler, 7 May 2003.

[11] See chapter 9 footnote #3 for a list of Sunshine Division commanders to the present.

[12] Captain Walter A. Tyler, "Their Sunshine" *Oregon Journal,* 8 June 1942.

[13] "Annual Report, The Sunshine Division of the City of Portland, 1943," City of Portland, SPARC, SSD Collection, A2000-026.

[14] Carl Abbott, *Portland: Planning Politics and Growth in a Twentieth Century City.* (Lincoln and London: University of Nebraska Press, 1983), 126.

Chapter 9 — Full Circle

[1] Ralph O'Hara, Interview with Lori Shea Kuechler, 7 May 2003.

[2] "SSD Boards, Commissions, Councils," General Board Minutes, Agendas, 1950–1974, Box 1, 17-06-15/3, 8023-06. City of Portland, SPARC, SSD Collection, A2000-026.

[3] "Portland Police Sunshine Division Commanders," Administrative Information, City of Portland, SPARC. The official list of commanders appointed by the Police Bureau to the Sunshine Division is as follows:
Captain Carroll H. Tichenor, June 30, 1922–May 1, 1942
Captain Walter A. Tyler, May 27, 1942–September 1, 1949
Captain Harry A. Circle, September 1, 1949–July 1, 1952
Sergeant Hugh A. Davenport, March 16, 1953–June 12, 1963
Sergeant Leland S. Lewis, June 13, 1963–September 12, 1973
Sergeant Frank E. Trout, November 1, 1973–July 28, 1975
Sergeant Paul A. Bonar, July 28, 1975–September 1, 1976
Sergeant Michael Salmon, August 5, 1976–July 13, 1990
Sergeant Jeanne Bradley, July 18, 1990–July 1, 1994
Sergeant Dick Gerety, February 9, 1995–December 27, 1995
Sergeant Karl McDade, March 7, 1996–February 18, 1998
Sergeant Wayne R. Kuechler, February 19, 1998–present

[4] "Annual Reports" 1940s, City of Portland, SPARC, SSD Collection, A2000-026.

[5] Edward Reid, "Police to Retire, Ending Half-Century Era," *Oregonian Journal,* 13 April 1952.

[6] The Sunshine Division has situated itself in four official locations. From the early twenties until 1927, it was located at 321 Belmont; from 1927 to 1938, 636 Southeast Alder; from 1938 to 1974, the Old Albina Police Precinct at 39 Northeast Russell Avenue; and finally, from 1974 to the present, an old machinery workshop purchased from the city for $1.00 at 638 North Thompson Street.

[7] Wayne R. Kuechler, Commander Portland Police Sunshine Division, Interview with Lori Shea Kuechler, 6 June 2003.

INDEX